UNICODE

Herong's Tutorial Examples

Unicode
Tutorials

Herong Yang
HerongYang.com/Unicode

Unicode Tutorials -

Herong's Tutorial Examples

v5.32, 2024

Herong Yang

This Unicode tutorial book is a collection of notes and sample codes written by the author while he was learning Unicode himself. Topics include Character Sets and Encodings; GB2312/GB18030 Character Set and Encodings; JIS X0208 Character Set and Encodings; Unicode Character Set; Basic Multilingual Plane (BMP); Unicode Transformation Formats (UTF); Surrogates and Supplementary Characters; Unicode Character Blocks; Python Support of Unicode Characters; Java Character Set and Encoding; Java Encoding Maps, Counts and Conversion. Updated in 2024 (Version v5.32) with minor changes.

Table of Contents

Keywords: Unicode, Universal, Character, Encoding, Tutorial, Book

About This Book

This section provides some detailed information about this book - Unicode Tutorials - Herong's Tutorial Examples.

Title: Unicode Tutorials - Herong's Tutorial Examples

Author: Herong Yang - Contact by email via herong_yang@yahoo.com.

Category: COMPUTERS / General

Version/Edition: v5.32, 2024

Number of pages in PDF format: 210

Description: This Unicode tutorial book is a collection of notes and sample codes written by the author while he was learning Unicode himself. Topics include Character Sets and Encodings; GB2312/GB18030 Character Set and Encodings; JIS X0208 Character Set and Encodings; Unicode Character Set; Basic Multilingual Plane (BMP); Unicode Transformation Formats (UTF); Surrogates and Supplementary Characters; Unicode Character Blocks; Python Support of Unicode Characters; Java Character Set and Encoding; Java Encoding Maps, Counts and Conversion. Updated in 2024 (Version v5.32) with minor changes.

Keywords: ASCII, BMP, character set, encoding, decoding, GB, GB18030, GB2312, GBK, ISO-8859, Java, JDK, JIS, Surrogate, UTF, Unicode.

Copyright:

Revision history:

- Version 5.31, 2022. Minor updates

- Version 5.30, 2020. Updated to Unicode 13.0.

- Version 5.20, 2019. Updated to Unicode 8.0.

- Version 5.00, 2009. Reformatted in hyPub format.

- Version 4.00, 2005. Added GB18030 tutorials.

- Version 3.00, 2001. Updated to Unicode 3.0.

- Version 2.00, 1997. Added GB2312 tutorials.

- Version 1.00, 1995. Started with character encoding tutorials.

Web version: https://www.herongyang.com/Unicode - Provides free sample chapters, latest updates and readers' comments. The Web version of this book has been viewed a total of:

- 2,214,097 times as of December 2021.

- 1,975,864 times as of December 2020.

- 1,742,803 times as of December 2019.

- 1,552,869 times as of December 2018.

- 1,338,708 times as of December 2017.

- 1,161,476 times as of December 2016.

- 990,563 times as of December 2015.

- 778,954 times as of December 2014.

- 555,987 times as of December 2013.

- 365,209 times as of December 2012.

- 211,527 times as of December 2011.

- 116,668 times as of December 2010.

- 78,928 times as of December 2009.

PDF/EPUB version: https://www.herongyang.com/Unicode/PDF-Full-Version.html - Provides information on how to obtain the full version of this book in PDF, EPUB, or other format.

Related Book:

- *Unicode Blocks - Herong's Notes*, Herong Yang, herongyang.com/Unicode-Blocks

- *GB2312 Tutorials - Herong's Tutorial Examples*, Herong Yang, herongyang.com/ GB2312

Character Sets and Encodings

This chapter provides notes and tutorial examples on character sets and encodings. Topics including introduction of character set and encoding; commonly used character sets and encodings.

Conclusions:

- A character set is a collection of characters.

- A character encoding a schema that maps each character in a character set to a unique sequence of bytes.

- Unicode is a character set.

- UTF-8 is a character encoding for the Unicode character set.

What Is Character Set

This section provides a quick introduction of some basic concepts like character set, coded character set, code point, character encoding.

What Is a Character Set? A character set is a collection of characters used in the a language, and/or symbols used in a symbolic system. Examples of character set: numeric numbers, alphabetical letters, and Chinese characters.

What Is a Coded Character Set? A coded character set is a character set in which each character has an assigned integral number. Examples of coded character set: US-ASCII, EBCDIC, ISO-8859-1, GB2312-1980, and Unicode. Note that:

- If character set B is a super set of character set A, we say B is backward compatible with A.

- Since we are only interested in coded character sets, so from now on I will use the term "character set" as "coded character set".

What Is a Code Point? A code point is an integral number assigned to a character in a coded character set.

What Is a Character Encoding A character encoding is a map scheme between code points of a coded character set and sequences of bytes. Note that:

- One coded character set may have many character encodings.

- One coded character set must have at least one character encoding.

Commonly Used Character Sets and Encodings

This section provides a list of commonly used character sets and their encodings.

The following table summaries some commonly used character sets and encodings:

Character Set	Encoding	# of Bytes	Byte Type	Language
ASCII	ASCII	1	7-bit	English
Latin1	ISO-8859-1	1	8-bit	Latin languages
GB2312-1980	GB	1-2	8-bit	Chinese
GB2312-1980	EUC-CN	1-2	8-bit	Chinese
GB2312-1980	HZ	1-2	7-bit	Chinese
GBK	GBK	1-2	8-bit	Chinese
GB18030-2000	GB18030-2000	1-4	8-bit	Chinese
Big5	Big5	1-2	8-bit	Chinese
CNS 11643-1992	EUC-TW	1-4	8-bit	Chinese
JIS	EUC-JP	1-2	8-bit	Japanese
JIS	ISO-2022-JP	1-2	7-bit	Japanese
JIS	Shift-JIS	1-2	8-bit	Japanese
KS	EUC-KR	1-2	8-bit	Korean
KS	ISO-2022-KR	1-2	7-bit	Korean
Unicode 3.0	UTF-7	1-3	8-bit	Multilingual
Unicode 3.0	UTF-8	1-3	8-bit	Multilingual

Unicode 3.0	UTF-16BE	2	8-bit	Multilingual
Unicode 3.0	UTF-16LE	2	8-bit	Multilingual
Unicode 3.1	UTF-8	1-4	8-bit	Multilingual

ASCII Character Set and Encoding

This chapter provides notes and tutorial examples on ASCII character set and encoding. Topics including introduction of ASCII (American Standard Code for Information Interchange); listing of all ASCII characters and their encoded bytes.

Conclusions:

• ASCII character set contains 128 characters for English letters, numbers and some control characters.

• ASCII encoding maps each character to 1 byte with the leading bit set to 0, and other 7 bits representing the code point of the character.

What Is ASCII

This section provides a quick introduction of ASCII (American Standard Code for Information Interchange) character set and encoding.

Before we jump into Unicode character set and Unicode encodings, we should first look at a much older and simpler character set, ASCII.

What Is ASCII? ASCII (American Standard Code for Information Interchange) is a character set and an encoding schema for English letters, numbers and some control characters.

The ASCII specification was published as "American Standard Code for Information Interchange, ASA X3.4-1963" by American Standards Association, in June 17, 1963.

The ASCII character set contains 95 printable characters and 33 control characters, giving a total of 128 characters. Their code points are integers range from 0 to 127, which can be mapped to 7 bits in binary format.

The ASCII encoding is simple, each character is mapped to 1 byte with the leading bit set to 0 and other 7 bits representing the character's code point as an integer.

Here is a picture of an ASCII code chart:

USASCII code chart

ASCII Code Chat

Listing of ASCII Characters and Encoded Bytes

This section provides a complete list of ASCII characters, code points and encoded bytes.

Here is complete list of ASCII characters, code points and encoding byte values:

Code Point	Encoded Byte (HEX)	Shot Name	Long Name
0	00	NUL	Null character
1	01	SOH	Start of Header
2	02	STX	Start of Text
3	03	ETX	End of Text
4	04	EOT	End of Transmission
5	05	ENQ	Enquiry
6	06	ACK	Acknowledgment
7	07	BEL	Bell

8	08	BS	Backspace
9	09	HT	Horizontal Tab
10	0A	LF	Line feed
11	0B	VT	Vertical Tab
12	0C	FF	Form feed
13	0D	CR	Carriage return
14	0E	SO	Shift Out
15	0F	SI	Shift In
16	10	DLE	Data Link Escape
17	11	DC1	Device Control 1 (oft. XON)
18	12	DC2	Device Control 2
19	13	DC3	Device Control 3 (oft. XOFF)
20	14	DC4	Device Control 4
21	15	NAK	Negative Acknowledgement
22	16	SYN	Synchronous Idle
23	17	ETB	End of Trans. Block
24	18	CAN	Cancel
25	19	EM	End of Medium
26	1A	SUB	Substitute
27	1B	ESC	Escape
28	1C	FS	File Separator
29	1D	GS	Group Separator
30	1E	RS	Record Separator
31	1F	US	Unit Separator
32	20		Printable character ?
33	21	!	Printable character !
34	22	"	Printable character "
35	23	#	Printable character #
36	24	$	Printable character $
37	25	%	Printable character %
38	26	&	Printable character &
39	27	'	Printable character '
40	28	(	Printable character (
41	29	)	Printable character)
42	2A	*	Printable character *
43	2B	+	Printable character +
44	2C	,	Printable character ,

45	2D	-	Printable character -
46	2E	.	Printable character .
47	2F	/	Printable character /
48	30	0	Printable character 0
49	31	1	Printable character 1
50	32	2	Printable character 2
51	33	3	Printable character 3
52	34	4	Printable character 4
53	35	5	Printable character 5
54	36	6	Printable character 6
55	37	7	Printable character 7
56	38	8	Printable character 8
57	39	9	Printable character 9
58	3A	:	Printable character :
59	3B	;	Printable character ;
60	3C	<	Printable character <
61	3D	=	Printable character =
62	3E	>	Printable character >
63	3F	?	Printable character ?
64	40	@	Printable character @
65	41	A	Printable character A
66	42	B	Printable character B
67	43	C	Printable character C
68	44	D	Printable character D
69	45	E	Printable character E
70	46	F	Printable character F
71	47	G	Printable character G
72	48	H	Printable character H
73	49	I	Printable character I
74	4A	J	Printable character J
75	4B	K	Printable character K
76	4C	L	Printable character L
77	4D	M	Printable character M
78	4E	N	Printable character N
79	4F	O	Printable character O
80	50	P	Printable character P
81	51	Q	Printable character Q

82	52	R	Printable character R
83	53	S	Printable character S
84	54	T	Printable character T
85	55	U	Printable character U
86	56	V	Printable character V
87	57	W	Printable character W
88	58	X	Printable character X
89	59	Y	Printable character Y
90	5A	Z	Printable character Z
91	5B	[	Printable character [
92	5C	\	Printable character \
93	5D	]	Printable character]
94	5E	^	Printable character ^
95	5F	_	Printable character _
96	60	`	Printable character `
97	61	a	Printable character a
98	62	b	Printable character b
99	63	c	Printable character c
100	64	d	Printable character d
101	65	e	Printable character e
102	66	f	Printable character f
103	67	g	Printable character g
104	68	h	Printable character h
105	69	i	Printable character i
106	6A	j	Printable character j
107	6B	k	Printable character k
108	6C	l	Printable character l
109	6D	m	Printable character m
110	6E	n	Printable character n
111	6F	o	Printable character o
112	70	p	Printable character p
113	71	q	Printable character q
114	72	r	Printable character r
115	73	s	Printable character s
116	74	t	Printable character t
117	75	u	Printable character u
118	76	v	Printable character v

119	77	w	Printable character w
120	78	x	Printable character x
121	79	y	Printable character y
122	7A	z	Printable character z
123	7B	{	Printable character {
124	7C	|	Printable character |
125	7D	}	Printable character }
126	7E	~	Printable character ~
127	7F	DEL	Delete

GB2312 Character Set and Encoding

This chapter provides notes and tutorial examples on GB2312 character set and encoding. Topics including introduction of the GB2312 character set for simplified Chinese characters; GB2312 encoding for the GB2312 character set; Relation of GB2312 and Unicode.

Conclusions:

- GB2312 character set contains 7445 simplified Chinese characters, numbers and symbols.

- GB2312 character set arranges characters into a matrix of 94 rows and 94 columns.

- GB2312 encoding uses 2 bytes: the high byte is the row number plus 158 and the low byte is the column number plus 158.

- GB2312 character set is a sub set of Unicode character set.

GB2312 Character Set for Chinese Characters

This section provides a quick introduction of the GB2312 character set for simplified Chinese characters, numbers and symbols. GB2312 contains 7445 characters.

GB: An abbreviation of Guojia Biaozhun, or Guo Biao, meaning "national standard" in Chinese.

GB2312, also called GB2312-1980: A coded character set established by the government of People's Republic of China (PRC) in 1980.

Main features of GB2312-1980:

- It contains 7445 characters, including 6763 Hanzi and 682 non-Hanzi characters.

- It is for simplified Chinese characters only. The traditional Chinese characters are included in Big5 character set.

- It is used mainly in China and Singapore.

GB2312-1980 arranges characters into a matrix of 94 rows and 94 columns. The rows are called quwei, and are organized as follows:

```
Rows        # of

Qu Wei      Chars    Characters


01           94      Special symbols
02           72      Paragraph numbers
03           94      GB 1988-80 (ISO 646-CN)
04           83      Hiragana
05           86      Katakana
06           48      Greek
07           66      Cyrillic
08           63      Pinyin accented vowels and zhuyin symbols
09           76      Box and table drawing pieces
16-55      3755      Hanzi level 1, ordered by pinyin
56-87      3008      Hanzi level 2, ordered by radical, then stroke
```

GB2312-1980 is a Double-Byte Character Set (DBCS), in which code point values requires 2-byte integers to hold. This is very different than the ASCII and Latin 1 character sets where every code point value can be hold by a 1-byte integer.

GB2312 Encoding for GB2312 Character Set

This section provides a quick introduction of the GB2312 encoding for the GB2312 character set. GB2312 is a 2-byte (8 bits per bytes) encoding.

GB2312 encoding is the main encoding for the GB2312 character set. GB2312 encoding is based on native code values of GB2312 characters.

The native code value of each GB2312 character contains 2 bytes. The first byte is called the high byte, containing the row number plus 32; the second byte is called the low byte, containing the column number plus 32. For example, if a character is located at row 16 and column 1, its high byte will be 16 + 32 = 48 (0x30), and log byte will be 1 + 32 = 33 (0x21). Put them together, its native code value will be 0x3021.

I guess that the reason to add 32 on both the row number and the column number is for the byte value to not fall into the low value range, which is usually reserved to represent controlling commands in many computer systems.

However, byte values of GB2312 native codes are not directly used as GB2312 encoding byte sequences, because they are still colliding with ASCII encoding types. To resolve this problem, a value of 128 is added to both bytes of native codes. For example, if a character is located at row 16 and column 1, its native code will be 0x3021, and its modified code will be 0xB0A1.

These modified codes are adopted as the GB2312 encoding, which can be safely mixed together with the ASCII encoding.

GB2312 encoding is also called EUC-CN (Extended Unix Code for China).

GB2312 character set has another encoding called HZ, which maps each GB2312 character to 2 7-bit bytes uses ~{...~} to separate GB2312 characters from ASCII characters.

Relation of GB2312 and Unicode

This section provides a quick introduction of the relation between GB2312 character set and Unicode character set.

GB2312 character set is sub set of Unicode character set. This means that every character defined in GB2312 is also defined in Unicode.

However, GB2312 codes and Unicode codes are totally un-related. For example, GB2312 character with code value of 0xB0A1 has a Unicode code value of 0x554A. There is no mathematical formula to convert a GB2312 code to a Unicode code of the same character.

My other tutorial book "Herong's Tutorial Notes on GB2312 Character Set" provides you a complete map of all GB2312 codes and their corresponding Unicode codes.

GB18030 Character Set and Encoding

This chapter provides notes and tutorial examples on GB18030 character set and encoding. Topics including history of GB character sets: GB2312, GB1300.1 (GBK) and GB18030; GB18030 encoding schema.

Conclusions:

- GBK (GB1300.1) is a super set of GB2312 with 21886 characters.

- GB18030 is a super set of GBK with 70244 characters.

- GB18030 character set is compatible with Unicode 3.0 character set.

- GB18030 encoding uses one, two or four bytes to encode a character.

History of GB Character Sets

This section provides a quick introduction of GB character sets: GB2312-1980, GB1300.1 and GB18030-2000.

GB: An abbreviation of Guojia Biaozhun, or Guo Biao, meaning "national standard" in Chinese.

GB2312-1980: A coded character set and encoding scheme established by the government of People's Republic of China (PRC) in 1980. GB2312-1980 contains 7445 characters, including 6763 Hanzi and 682 non-Hanzi characters.

GB1300.1: A coded character set and encoding scheme established by the government of PRC in 1993 for Hanzi characters. GB1300.1 is designed to be compatible with Unicode 2.1 by maintaining all characters in GB2312-1980 untouched, and positioning all additional characters defined in the Unified Han portion of Unicode 2.1 around the

GB2312-1980 character set. GB1300.1 is also called Guojia Biaozhun Kuozhan (GBK). It defines 23940 code points containing 21886 characters.

GB18030-2000: A coded character set and encoding scheme established by PRC as an update of GB1300.1 to be compatible with Unicode 3.0. GB18030-2000 has 1.6 million valid code points, 0.5 million more than Unicode 3.0.

The government of PRC has required, since September 1, 2001, that all operating systems on non-handheld computers sold in PRC must comply with the GB18030-2000 standard.

GB18030 Encoding for GB18030 Character Set

This section provides a quick introduction of the GB18030 encoding for the GB18030 character set. GB18030 is a multi-byte (1-byte, 2-byte, or 4-byte) encoding.

GB18030 encoding scheme uses one, two or four bytes to encode a character. The following table shows the ranges of valid byte sequences:

Number Of Bytes	Valid Range Byte 1	Byte 2	Byte 3	Byte 4
1	0x00 - 0x7F			
2	0x81 - 0xFE	0x40 - 0x7E		
2	0x81 - 0xFE	0x80 - 0xFE		
4	0x81 - 0xFE	0x30 - 0x39	0x81 - 0xFE	0x30 - 0x39

Processing a GB18030 encoded byte stream from the beginning of the stream is easy. Here is an algorithm to divide the stream into sequences of bytes that represent valid GB18030 characters:

```
Input:
   byte stream in
Algorithm:
   while (in.hasNext())
      b1 = in.nextByte()
      if (0x00 <= b1 && b1 <= 0x7F)
         b1 is a valid byte sequence
```

```
      else if (0x81 <= b1 && b1 <= 0xFE && in.hasNext())
         b2 = in.nextByte()
         if ((0x40 <= b2 && b2 <= 0x7E) || (0x80 <= b2 && b2 <= 0xFE))
            b1, b2 is a valid byte sequence
         else if (0x30 <= b2 && b2 <= 0x39 && in.hasNext())
            b3 = in.nextByte()
            if (0x81 <= b3 && b3 <= 0xFE && in.hasNext())
               b4 = in.nextByte()
               if (0x30 <= b4 && b4 <= 0x39)
                  b1, b2, b3, b4 is a valid byte sequence
               else
                  stream is corrupted
               end if
            else
               stream is corrupted
            end if
         else
            stream is corrupted
         end if
      else
         stream is corrupted
      end if
   end while
```

Thanks to Mark, who provided suggestions to make the above algorithm more accurate.

JIS X0208 Character Set and Encodings

This chapter provides notes and tutorial examples on JIS X0208 character set and encodings. Topics including introduction of the JIS X0208 character set; EUC-JP, ISO-2022-JP and Shift-JIS encodings.

Conclusions:

- JIS X0208 is a character set for Japanese characters.

- JIS X0208 arranges characters into a matrix of 94 rows and 94 columns.

- The code value of a JIS X0208 character is a 2-byte value: the high byte is the row number plus 32 and low byte is the column number plus 32.

- EUC-JP is an encoding that maps a JIS X0208 character to a 2-byte sequence by adding 128 to each byte of the byte pair of the character's code value.

- ISO-2022-JP is an encoding that maps a JIS X0208 character to a 2-byte sequence by taking both bytes directly from the character's code value. Escape sequences are used to mix ASCII characters with JIS X0208 characters.

- Shift-JIS is an encoding developed by Microsoft for JIS X0208 characters.

JIS X0208 Character Set for Japanese Characters

This section provides a quick introduction of the JIS X0208 character set used for Japanese language characters.

JIS X0208: A coded character set established for Japanese in 1990. JIS stands for Japanese Industrial Standards.

JIS X0208 arranges characters into a matrix of 94 rows and 94 columns. The rows are called quwei, and are organized as follows:

```
Rows       # of
Qu Wei    Chars    Characters


01-02              Punctuation, symbols
03                 ISO 646 (alphanumerics only)
04                 Hiragana
05                 Katakana
06                 Greek
07                 Cyrillic
08                 Line drawing
16-47     2965     Kanji level 1, ordered by on-yomi
48-83     3384     Kanji level 2, ordered by Kangxi radical, then stroke
84           6     Miscellaneous kanji
```

There are four sub character sets used in writing modern Japanese: katakana, hiragana, kanji, and romaji.

Katakana contains 46 characters, with very angular strokes. Each Katakana character represents a unique sound. There are 5 vowels in them. Katakan characters can be used to express any sound in the Japanese language.

Katakana is like Pinyin in Chinese. It is commonly used to express foreign names.

Hiragana contains 46 characters, with very smoother strokes. Each Hiragana character represents a unique sound. Hiragana characters can be used to express any sound in the Japanese language. Hiragana is closely related to Katakana. In fact, each Hiragana character has a counterpart in Katakana.

Hiragana is commonly used to express simple words. It is also the first writing system taught to Japanese children.

Kanji contains thousands of Chinese characters, that were brought to Japan many years ago.

Romaji contains the Roman alphabets. Of course, they are used to express foreign words.

JIS X0208 Character Code Values

This section provides a quick introduction of JIS X0208 character code values. Each character has a code of 2 bytes: high byte is row number plus 32 and low byte is column number plus 32.

The native code value of each JIS X0208 character contains 2 bytes. The first byte is called the high byte, containing the row number plus 32 (0x20); the second byte is called the low byte, containing the column number plus 32 (0x20). For example, if a character is located at row 16 and column 1, its high byte will be 16 + 32 = 48 (0x30), and log byte will be 1 + 32 = 33 (0x21). Put them together, its native code value will be 0x3021.

The reason to add 32 to each byte of the code value is that the resulting byte value can be represented by a printable ASCII character, between 0x21 and 0x7f. In another word, the code value of any JIS X0208 character is a combination of 2 printable ASCII characters.

Below is a picture showing the location area of JIS X0208 character code values on a 2-byte value map, modified from http://lfw.org/text/jp.html:

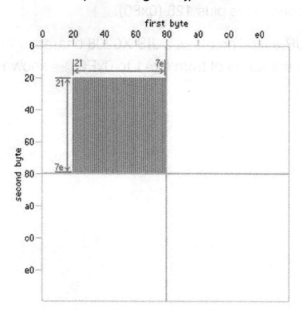

JIS X0208 Character Code Values

EUC-JP Encoding

This section provides a quick introduction of EUC-JP encoding, which maps a JIS X0208 character to a 2-byte sequence by adding 128 (0x80) to both bytes of the character's code value.

EUC-JP (Extended Unix Code for Japanese): An encoding for JIS X0208 character set. It is an 8-bit encoding with 1 or 2 bytes per character:

```
Number Of    Valid Range
Bytes        Byte 1          Byte 2


   1         0x21 - 0x7F
   2         0xA1 - 0xFE     0xA1 - 0xFE
```

Of course, 1-byte encoding sequences are used for ASCII characters.

2-byte encoding sequences are used for JIS X0208 characters. The mapping schema is simple. The first byte of a encoding sequence is the high byte value of the character code value plus 128 (0x80). The second byte of a encoding sequence is the low byte value of the character code value plus 128 (0x80).

In another word, EUC-JP encoding maps a JIS X0208 character to a 2-byte sequence with both byte values in the range of from 0xA1 to 0xFE, as shown in the picture below:

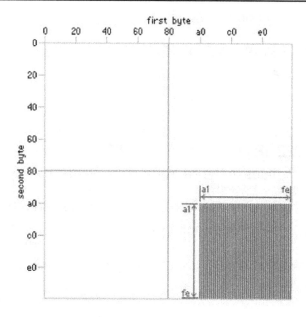

EUC-JP Encoding

The advantage of EUC-JP encoding is that ASCII characters and JIS X0208 characters can be mixed together without using any escape sequences.

The disadvantage of EUC-JP encoding is that it uses 8-bit bytes, which are not safe to transmit through many communication interfaces.

ISO-2022-JP Encoding

This section provides a quick introduction of ISO-2022-JP encoding, which maps a JIS X0208 character to a 2-byte sequence by using both bytes of the character's code value directly.

ISO-2022-JP: An encoding for JIS X0208 character set. It is a 7-bit encoding with 1 or 2 bytes per character:

Number Of Bytes	Valid Range Byte 1	Byte 2
1	0x21 - 0x7F	
2	0x21 - 0x7E	0x21 - 0x7E

Of course, 1-byte encoding sequences are used for ASCII characters.

2-byte encoding sequences are used for JIS X0208 characters. The mapping schema is simple. The first byte of a encoding sequence is the high byte value of the character code value. The second byte of a encoding sequence is the low byte value of the character code value.

In another word, ISO-2022-JP encoding maps a JIS X0208 character to a 2-byte sequence with both byte values in the range of from 0x21 to 0x7E.

Escape sequences are used to switch between the 1-byte sequence mode for ASCII characters and the 2-byte sequence mode for JIS X0208 characters:

```
<Esc>(J - Escape sequence for ASCII characters
<Esc>$B - Escape sequence for JIS X0208 characters
```

The advantage of ISO-2022-JP encoding is that it uses 7-bit bytes, which are safe to transmit through any communication interfaces.

The disadvantage of ISO-2022-JP encoding is that it uses escape sequences to mix ASCII characters with JIS X0208 characters.

Shift-JIS Encoding

This section provides a quick introduction of Shift-JIS, also called MS Kanji, encoding, which maps a JIS X0208 character to a 2-byte sequence using a complicated schema designed by Microsoft.

Shift-JIS: An encoding for JIS X0208 character set. It is a 8-bit encoding with 1 to 2 bytes per character:

```
Number Of    Valid Range
Bytes        Byte 1          Byte 2


   1         0x21 - 0x7F   (for ASCII)
   1         0xA1 - 0xDF (for Katakana)
   2         0x81 - 0x9F    0x40 - 0x7E
   2         0xE0 - 0xEF    0x80 - 0xFC
```

Shift-JIS, also called MS Kanji, is a Microsoft standard (codepage 932). The encoding schema is not straightforward. Please read http://en.wikipedia.org/wiki/Shift_JIS for more details.

Unicode Character Set

This chapter provides notes and tutorial examples on the Unicode character set. Topics including introduction of Unicode standard, example characters, history of releases, blocks of code points.

Conclusions:

- The latest major release of the Unicode standard is 8.0, which contains 120,737 characters.

- Each Unicode character has a code point and a code name.

- Unicode code points are numeric values in the range of 0x000000 and 0x10FFFF.

- Unicode is compatible with the ISO/IEC 10646 standard.

What Is Unicode

This section provides a quick introduction of the Unicode character set, which contains all characters used in all written languages of the world.

Unicode is a coded character set that contains all characters used in all written languages of the world. It also contains many symbols.

Unicode is fully compatible with the ISO/IEC 10646 standard.

Glyph: A visual representation of one fundamental element of written languages or symbols printed on paper or screen. For example, the letter "Z" is a glyph; and the letter "a" with "^" on top is another glyph.

Glyph is a measurement of shapes and forms of a language. Glyphs are font dependent, the same letter can be display with different glyphs, if different fonts is used.

Code Element: A digital representation of one fundamental semantic value of written languages and symbols. For example, the letter "Z", no matter how many different forms and shape it can be printed on paper or screen, it only has one semantic value - the capital letter "Z". So it can be represented by one code element. Another example is the letter "a" with "^" on top. Semantically, it may be represented by two values: the small letter "a" and the circumflex accent "^". So it can be represented by two code elements.

Character: Same as code element in Unicode context. But in other contexts, a character might be a larger measurement. For example, the letter "a" with "^" on top, is called one character in many non-Unicode contexts, but it is represented by two code elements, or two characters in Unicode context.

Code Point: A unique number assigned to a code element, usually represented in hexadecimal form with the prefix of "U+". For example, the code point of code element for the letter "Z" in Latin language is U+005A; and the code point of code element for the circumflex accent is U+0302.

Code Name: A name assigned to a code element. Code names used in Unicode are compatible with character names defined in ISO/IEC 10646.

Putting all those concepts together, now we can say that Unicode is a character set, in which, each character has:

- A Code Element - A long description that defines the character.

- A Code Name - A short term that names the character.

- A Code Point - A numeric value that represents the character.

Examples of Unicode Characters

Some samples of Unicode characters are provided here with their glyphs, code points, code names and code blocks for the purpose of demonstration.

Samples of Unicode characters with their glyphs, code points, code names and code blocks:

```
Glyph Code      Code
      Point     Name


z     U+0005A LATIN CAPITAL LEETER Z
              Code Block: Basic Latin


a     U+00061 LATIN SMALL LETTER A
              Code Block: Basic Latin


â     U+000E2 LATIN SMALL LETTER A WITH CIRCUMFLEX
              Code Block: Latin-1 Supplement


©     U+000A9 COPYRIGHT SIGN
              Code Block: Latin-1 Supplement


Δ     U+00394 GREEK CAPITAL LETTER DELTA
              Code Block: Greek and Coptic


°       U+0110B HANGUL CHOSEONG IEUNG
              Code Block: Hangul Jamo


      U+020AC EURO SIGN
              Code Block: Currency Symbols
```

```
山      U+05C71 Chinese character for mountain
            Code Block: CJK Unified Ideographs
```

Unique Features of Unicode

This section provides summary of unique features of the Unicode standard.

Comparing with other character coding standard, Unicode has the following unique features:

- Full 16-bit coding. Each code is 16-bit number. No restriction. None of the 16 bits is reserved for any special purposes.

- Big enough to handle all existing written languages and symbols. 16 bits gives 65536 code values. It can be expended to paired 16-bit codes to cover millions of code values.

- Characters in the same language are coded in groups and ordered according their natural sequence whenever it's possible.

- No escape sequences. No shift states.

- Common characters (letters) in languages are unified into code element. The biggest example is the unification of Chinese/Japanese/Korean (CJK) ideographs into one common set of code elements.

Another interesting feature of Unicode is the use of equivalent sequences. Different sequences of code elements that represent the same semantic value are called equivalent sequences. For example, the small letter "a" and the circumflex accent "^" can be represented by a single code element: U+00E2 (LATIN SMALL LETTER A WITH CIRCUMFLEX). It can also be represented by a sequence of two code elements: U+0302 (COMBINING CIRCUMFLEX ACCENT) and U+0061 (LATIN SMALL LETTER A). So U+00E2 and U+0302U+0061 are equivalent sequences. See the demonstration table below:

```
1. U+00E2              = â
2. U+0302U+0061        = â
```

```
3.  U+0061U+0302       = a^
4.  U+0061U+0302U+0062 = ab̂
5.  U+0062U+0302U+0061 = b̂a
6.  U+0062U+0302U+0066 = bf̂
```

The above table shows how a Web browser handles a sequence that has a "combining" element:

- The "combining" element will be combined with the next element or the previous element depending on which element can accept the "combining" element, see line 2, 3, 4 and 5 in the table.

- If both the next element and the previous element are not suitable for the "combining" element, it will be forcibly combined with the next element, see line 6 in the table.

Note that when send the same table to a PDF generation tool, "combining" sequences may not be respected.

Unicode Standard Releases

This section provides a list of major releases of the Unicode standard and their publishing dates.

Since its first release in 1991, Unicode standard has gone through a number releases, Here is a list Unicode major releases.

Unicode 15.0.0 - Published in September 13, 2022 as a book called "Unicode 15.0.0" at unicode.org/versions/Unicode15.0.0/. Unicode 15.0 added 4,489 characters, for a total of 149,186 characters. These additions include 2 new scripts, for a total of 161 scripts, along with 20 new emoji characters, and 4,193 CJK (Chinese, Japanese, and Korean) ideographs.

Unicode 14.0.0 - Published in September 14, 2021 as a book called "Unicode 14.0.0" at unicode.org/versions/Unicode14.0.0/. Unicode 14.0 added 838 characters, for a total of 144,697 characters. These additions include 5 new scripts, for a total of 159 scripts, as well as 37 new emoji characters.

Unicode 13.0.0 - Published in March 10, 2020 as a book called "Unicode 13.0.0" at unicode.org/versions/Unicode13.0.0/. Unicode 13.0 added 5,930 characters, for a total of 143,859 characters. These additions include 4 new scripts, for a total of 154 scripts, as well as 55 new emoji characters.

Unicode 12.0.0 - Published in March 5, 2019 as a book called "Unicode 12.0.0" at unicode.org/versions/Unicode12.0.0/. Unicode 12.0 added 554 characters, for a total of 137,928 character. These additions include 4 new scripts, for a total of 150 scripts, as well as 61 new emoji characters.

Unicode 11.0.0 - Published in June, 2018 as a book called "The Unicode Standard, Version 11.0.0" (ISBN 978-1-936213-19-1) at unicode.org/versions/Unicode11.0.0/. Unicode 11.0 added 684 characters, for a total of 137,374 characters. These additions include 7 new scripts, for a total of 146 scripts, as well as 66 new emoji characters.

Unicode 10.0.0 - Published in June, 2017 as a book called "The Unicode Standard, Version 10.0.0" (ISBN 978-1-936213-16-0) at unicode.org/versions/Unicode10.0.0/. Unicode 10.0 added 8,518 characters, for a total of 136,690 characters. These additions include 4 new scripts, for a total of 139 scripts, as well as 56 new emoji characters.

Unicode 9.0.0 - Published in June, 2016 as a book called "The Unicode Standard, Version 9.0.0" (ISBN 978-1-936213-13-9) at unicode.org/versions/Unicode9.0.0/. Unicode 9.0 added 7,500 characters, for a total of 128,172 characters. These additions include six new scripts and 72 new emoji characters.

Unicode 8.0.0 - Published in June, 2015 as a book called "The Unicode Standard, Version 8.0.0" (ISBN 978-1-936213-10-8). Unicode 8.0 added a total of 7,716 characters, encompassing six new scripts and many new symbols, as well as character additions to several existing scripts. There are 120,737 characters defined in Unicode 8.0.

Unicode 7.0.0 - Published in June, 2014 as a book called "he Unicode Standard, Version 8.0.0" (ISBN 978-1-936213-09-2). Unicode 7.0 added a total of 2,834 characters, encompassing 23 new scripts and many new symbols, as well as character additions to many existing scripts.

Unicode 6.0.0 - Published in February, 2011 as a book called "The Unicode Standard Version 6.0 - Core Specification" (ISBN 978-1-936213-01-6). Unicode 6.0 contains 109,449 characters from the world's scripts.

Unicode 5.1.0 - Published in April, 2008 as a technical report which added 1,624 new characters.

Unicode 5.0.0 - Published in July, 2006 as a book called "The Unicode Standard, Version 5.0" (ISBN 0-321-48091-0). Unicode 5.0 contains 99,024 characters from the world's scripts.

Unicode 4.1.0 - Published in March, 2005 as technical report which added 1,273 new characters.

Unicode 4.0.0 - Published in April, 2003 as a book called "The Unicode Standard, Version 4.0" (ISBN 0-321-18578-1). Unicode 4.0 contains 96,382 characters from the world's scripts.

Unicode 3.2.0 - Published in March, 2002 as technical report which added 1,016 new characters in the Basic Multilingual Plane (BMP), U+0000...U+FFFF.

Unicode 3.1.0 - Published in March, 2001 as technical report which added 44,946 new characters and extended code point value beyond the original 2-byte boundary. New characters are added with code points in U+10000...U+2FFFF and U+E0000...U+EFFFF ranges.

Unicode 3.0.0 - Published in September, 1999 as a book called "The Unicode Standard, Version 3.0" (ISBN 0-201-61633-5). Unicode 3.0 contains 49,194 characters from the world's scripts.

Unicode 2.1.0 - Published in 1998 as a technical report which fixed a number of errors, added the U+20AC EURO SIGN for the new European currency, and so on.

Unicode 2.0.0 - Published in July, 1996 as a book called "The Unicode Standard, Version 2.0" (ISBN 0-201-48345-9).

Unicode 1.1.0 - Published in June, 1993 as two proposals. Unicode 1.1.0 is compatible with the international standard, ISO/IEC 10646 - Universal Multiple-Octet Coded Character Set (UCS).

Unicode 1.0.0 - Published in October, 1991 as a book called "The Unicode Standard, Version 1.0" (ISBN 0-201-56788-1).

Code Point Blocks

This section provides a list of major releases of the Unicode standard and their publishing dates.

Unicode code points are organized into blocks. Here is a list of code point blocks defined in Unicode 15.0.0:

```
    Start           End
    Code           Code
    Point          Point      Block Name
--------- ...   --------      ----------
  U+0000 ...     U+007F      Basic Latin
  U+0080 ...     U+00FF      Latin-1 Supplement
  U+0100 ...     U+017F      Latin Extended-A
  U+0180 ...     U+024F      Latin Extended-B
  U+0250 ...     U+02AF      IPA Extensions
  U+02B0 ...     U+02FF      Spacing Modifier Letters
  U+0300 ...     U+036F      Combining Diacritical Marks
  U+0370 ...     U+03FF      Greek and Coptic
  U+0400 ...     U+04FF      Cyrillic
  U+0500 ...     U+052F      Cyrillic Supplement
  U+0530 ...     U+058F      Armenian
  U+0590 ...     U+05FF      Hebrew
  U+0600 ...     U+06FF      Arabic
  U+0700 ...     U+074F      Syriac
  U+0750 ...     U+077F      Arabic Supplement
  U+0780 ...     U+07BF      Thaana
  U+07C0 ...     U+07FF      NKo
  U+0800 ...     U+083F      Samaritan
  U+0840 ...     U+085F      Mandaic
  U+0860 ...     U+086F      Syriac Supplement
  U+0870 ...     U+089F      Arabic Extended-B
  U+08A0 ...     U+08FF      Arabic Extended-A
  U+0900 ...     U+097F      Devanagari
  U+0980 ...     U+09FF      Bengali
  U+0A00 ...     U+0A7F      Gurmukhi
  U+0A80 ...     U+0AFF      Gujarati
  U+0B00 ...     U+0B7F      Oriya
  U+0B80 ...     U+0BFF      Tamil
  U+0C00 ...     U+0C7F      Telugu
  U+0C80 ...     U+0CFF      Kannada
  U+0D00 ...     U+0D7F      Malayalam
```

U+0D80 ...	U+0DFF	Sinhala
U+0E00 ...	U+0E7F	Thai
U+0E80 ...	U+0EFF	Lao
U+0F00 ...	U+0FFF	Tibetan
U+1000 ...	U+109F	Myanmar
U+10A0 ...	U+10FF	Georgian
U+1100 ...	U+11FF	Hangul Jamo
U+1200 ...	U+137F	Ethiopic
U+1380 ...	U+139F	Ethiopic Supplement
U+13A0 ...	U+13FF	Cherokee
U+1400 ...	U+167F	Unified Canadian Aboriginal Syllabics
U+1680 ...	U+169F	Ogham
U+16A0 ...	U+16FF	Runic
U+1700 ...	U+171F	Tagalog
U+1720 ...	U+173F	Hanunoo
U+1740 ...	U+175F	Buhid
U+1760 ...	U+177F	Tagbanwa
U+1780 ...	U+17FF	Khmer
U+1800 ...	U+18AF	Mongolian
U+18B0 ...	U+18FF	Unified Canadian Aboriginal Syllabics Extended
U+1900 ...	U+194F	Limbu
U+1950 ...	U+197F	Tai Le
U+1980 ...	U+19DF	New Tai Lue
U+19E0 ...	U+19FF	Khmer Symbols
U+1A00 ...	U+1A1F	Buginese
U+1A20 ...	U+1AAF	Tai Tham
U+1AB0 ...	U+1AFF	Combining Diacritical Marks Extended
U+1B00 ...	U+1B7F	Balinese
U+1B80 ...	U+1BBF	Sundanese
U+1BC0 ...	U+1BFF	Batak
U+1C00 ...	U+1C4F	Lepcha
U+1C50 ...	U+1C7F	Ol Chiki
U+1C80 ...	U+1C8F	Cyrillic Extended-C
U+1C90 ...	U+1CBF	Georgian Extended
U+1CC0 ...	U+1CCF	Sundanese Supplement
U+1CD0 ...	U+1CFF	Vedic Extensions
U+1D00 ...	U+1D7F	Phonetic Extensions

U+1D80 ...	U+1DBF	Phonetic Extensions Supplement
U+1DC0 ...	U+1DFF	Combining Diacritical Marks Supplement
U+1E00 ...	U+1EFF	Latin Extended Additional
U+1F00 ...	U+1FFF	Greek Extended
U+2000 ...	U+206F	General Punctuation
U+2070 ...	U+209F	Superscripts and Subscripts
U+20A0 ...	U+20CF	Currency Symbols
U+20D0 ...	U+20FF	Combining Diacritical Marks for Symbols
U+2100 ...	U+214F	Letterlike Symbols
U+2150 ...	U+218F	Number Forms
U+2190 ...	U+21FF	Arrows
U+2200 ...	U+22FF	Mathematical Operators
U+2300 ...	U+23FF	Miscellaneous Technical
U+2400 ...	U+243F	Control Pictures
U+2440 ...	U+245F	Optical Character Recognition
U+2460 ...	U+24FF	Enclosed Alphanumerics
U+2500 ...	U+257F	Box Drawing
U+2580 ...	U+259F	Block Elements
U+25A0 ...	U+25FF	Geometric Shapes
U+2600 ...	U+26FF	Miscellaneous Symbols
U+2700 ...	U+27BF	Dingbats
U+27C0 ...	U+27EF	Miscellaneous Mathematical Symbols-A
U+27F0 ...	U+27FF	Supplemental Arrows-A
U+2800 ...	U+28FF	Braille Patterns
U+2900 ...	U+297F	Supplemental Arrows-B
U+2980 ...	U+29FF	Miscellaneous Mathematical Symbols-B
U+2A00 ...	U+2AFF	Supplemental Mathematical Operators
U+2B00 ...	U+2BFF	Miscellaneous Symbols and Arrows
U+2C00 ...	U+2C5F	Glagolitic
U+2C60 ...	U+2C7F	Latin Extended-C
U+2C80 ...	U+2CFF	Coptic
U+2D00 ...	U+2D2F	Georgian Supplement
U+2D30 ...	U+2D7F	Tifinagh
U+2D80 ...	U+2DDF	Ethiopic Extended
U+2DE0 ...	U+2DFF	Cyrillic Extended-A
U+2E00 ...	U+2E7F	Supplemental Punctuation
U+2E80 ...	U+2EFF	CJK Radicals Supplement

U+2F00 ...	U+2FDF	Kangxi Radicals
U+2FF0 ...	U+2FFF	Ideographic Description Characters
U+3000 ...	U+303F	CJK Symbols and Punctuation
U+3040 ...	U+309F	Hiragana
U+30A0 ...	U+30FF	Katakana
U+3100 ...	U+312F	Bopomofo
U+3130 ...	U+318F	Hangul Compatibility Jamo
U+3190 ...	U+319F	Kanbun
U+31A0 ...	U+31BF	Bopomofo Extended
U+31C0 ...	U+31EF	CJK Strokes
U+31F0 ...	U+31FF	Katakana Phonetic Extensions
U+3200 ...	U+32FF	Enclosed CJK Letters and Months
U+3300 ...	U+33FF	CJK Compatibility
U+3400 ...	U+4DBF	CJK Unified Ideographs Extension A
U+4DC0 ...	U+4DFF	Yijing Hexagram Symbols
U+4E00 ...	U+9FFF	CJK Unified Ideographs
U+A000 ...	U+A48F	Yi Syllables
U+A490 ...	U+A4CF	Yi Radicals
U+A4D0 ...	U+A4FF	Lisu
U+A500 ...	U+A63F	Vai
U+A640 ...	U+A69F	Cyrillic Extended-B
U+A6A0 ...	U+A6FF	Bamum
U+A700 ...	U+A71F	Modifier Tone Letters
U+A720 ...	U+A7FF	Latin Extended-D
U+A800 ...	U+A82F	Syloti Nagri
U+A830 ...	U+A83F	Common Indic Number Forms
U+A840 ...	U+A87F	Phags-pa
U+A880 ...	U+A8DF	Saurashtra
U+A8E0 ...	U+A8FF	Devanagari Extended
U+A900 ...	U+A92F	Kayah Li
U+A930 ...	U+A95F	Rejang
U+A960 ...	U+A97F	Hangul Jamo Extended-A
U+A980 ...	U+A9DF	Javanese
U+A9E0 ...	U+A9FF	Myanmar Extended-B
U+AA00 ...	U+AA5F	Cham
U+AA60 ...	U+AA7F	Myanmar Extended-A
U+AA80 ...	U+AADF	Tai Viet

U+AAE0 ...	U+AAFF	Meetei Mayek Extensions
U+AB00 ...	U+AB2F	Ethiopic Extended-A
U+AB30 ...	U+AB6F	Latin Extended-E
U+AB70 ...	U+ABBF	Cherokee Supplement
U+ABC0 ...	U+ABFF	Meetei Mayek
U+AC00 ...	U+D7AF	Hangul Syllables
U+D7B0 ...	U+D7FF	Hangul Jamo Extended-B
U+D800 ...	U+DB7F	High Surrogates
U+DB80 ...	U+DBFF	High Private Use Surrogates
U+DC00 ...	U+DFFF	Low Surrogates
U+E000 ...	U+F8FF	Private Use Area
U+F900 ...	U+FAFF	CJK Compatibility Ideographs
U+FB00 ...	U+FB4F	Alphabetic Presentation Forms
U+FB50 ...	U+FDFF	Arabic Presentation Forms-A
U+FE00 ...	U+FE0F	Variation Selectors
U+FE10 ...	U+FE1F	Vertical Forms
U+FE20 ...	U+FE2F	Combining Half Marks
U+FE30 ...	U+FE4F	CJK Compatibility Forms
U+FE50 ...	U+FE6F	Small Form Variants
U+FE70 ...	U+FEFF	Arabic Presentation Forms-B
U+FF00 ...	U+FFEF	Halfwidth and Fullwidth Forms
U+FFF0 ...	U+FFFF	Specials
U+10000 ...	U+1007F	Linear B Syllabary
U+10080 ...	U+100FF	Linear B Ideograms
U+10100 ...	U+1013F	Aegean Numbers
U+10140 ...	U+1018F	Ancient Greek Numbers
U+10190 ...	U+101CF	Ancient Symbols
U+101D0 ...	U+101FF	Phaistos Disc
U+10280 ...	U+1029F	Lycian
U+102A0 ...	U+102DF	Carian
U+102E0 ...	U+102FF	Coptic Epact Numbers
U+10300 ...	U+1032F	Old Italic
U+10330 ...	U+1034F	Gothic
U+10350 ...	U+1037F	Old Permic
U+10380 ...	U+1039F	Ugaritic
U+103A0 ...	U+103DF	Old Persian
U+10400 ...	U+1044F	Deseret

U+10450 ...	U+1047F	Shavian
U+10480 ...	U+104AF	Osmanya
U+104B0 ...	U+104FF	Osage
U+10500 ...	U+1052F	Elbasan
U+10530 ...	U+1056F	Caucasian Albanian
U+10570 ...	U+105BF	Vithkuqi
U+10600 ...	U+1077F	Linear A
U+10780 ...	U+107BF	Latin Extended-F
U+10800 ...	U+1083F	Cypriot Syllabary
U+10840 ...	U+1085F	Imperial Aramaic
U+10860 ...	U+1087F	Palmyrene
U+10880 ...	U+108AF	Nabataean
U+108E0 ...	U+108FF	Hatran
U+10900 ...	U+1091F	Phoenician
U+10920 ...	U+1093F	Lydian
U+10980 ...	U+1099F	Meroitic Hieroglyphs
U+109A0 ...	U+109FF	Meroitic Cursive
U+10A00 ...	U+10A5F	Kharoshthi
U+10A60 ...	U+10A7F	Old South Arabian
U+10A80 ...	U+10A9F	Old North Arabian
U+10AC0 ...	U+10AFF	Manichaean
U+10B00 ...	U+10B3F	Avestan
U+10B40 ...	U+10B5F	Inscriptional Parthian
U+10B60 ...	U+10B7F	Inscriptional Pahlavi
U+10B80 ...	U+10BAF	Psalter Pahlavi
U+10C00 ...	U+10C4F	Old Turkic
U+10C80 ...	U+10CFF	Old Hungarian
U+10D00 ...	U+10D3F	Hanifi Rohingya
U+10E60 ...	U+10E7F	Rumi Numeral Symbols
U+10E80 ...	U+10EBF	Yezidi
U+10EC0 ...	U+10EFF	Arabic Extended-C
U+10F00 ...	U+10F2F	Old Sogdian
U+10F30 ...	U+10F6F	Sogdian
U+10F70 ...	U+10FAF	Old Uyghur
U+10FB0 ...	U+10FDF	Chorasmian
U+10FE0 ...	U+10FFF	Elymaic
U+11000 ...	U+1107F	Brahmi

```
U+11080 ...   U+110CF    Kaithi
U+110D0 ...   U+110FF    Sora Sompeng
U+11100 ...   U+1114F    Chakma
U+11150 ...   U+1117F    Mahajani

U+11180 ...   U+111DF    Sharada
U+111E0 ...   U+111FF    Sinhala Archaic Numbers
U+11200 ...   U+1124F    Khojki
U+11280 ...   U+112AF    Multani
U+112B0 ...   U+112FF    Khudawadi
U+11300 ...   U+1137F    Grantha
U+11400 ...   U+1147F    Newa
U+11480 ...   U+114DF    Tirhuta
U+11580 ...   U+115FF    Siddham
U+11600 ...   U+1165F    Modi
U+11660 ...   U+1167F    Mongolian Supplement
U+11680 ...   U+116CF    Takri
U+11700 ...   U+1174F    Ahom
U+11800 ...   U+1184F    Dogra
U+118A0 ...   U+118FF    Warang Citi
U+11900 ...   U+1195F    Dives Akuru
U+119A0 ...   U+119FF    Nandinagari
U+11A00 ...   U+11A4F    Zanabazar Square
U+11A50 ...   U+11AAF    Soyombo
U+11AB0 ...   U+11ABF    Unified Canadian Aboriginal Syllabics Extended-A
U+11AC0 ...   U+11AFF    Pau Cin Hau
U+11B00 ...   U+11B5F    Devanagari Extended-A
U+11C00 ...   U+11C6F    Bhaiksuki
U+11C70 ...   U+11CBF    Marchen
U+11D00 ...   U+11D5F    Masaram Gondi
U+11D60 ...   U+11DAF    Gunjala Gondi
U+11EE0 ...   U+11EFF    Makasar
U+11F00 ...   U+11F5F    Kawi
U+11FB0 ...   U+11FBF    Lisu Supplement
U+11FC0 ...   U+11FFF    Tamil Supplement
U+12000 ...   U+123FF    Cuneiform
U+12400 ...   U+1247F    Cuneiform Numbers and Punctuation
U+12480 ...   U+1254F    Early Dynastic Cuneiform
```

U+12F90 ...	U+12FFF	Cypro-Minoan
U+13000 ...	U+1342F	Egyptian Hieroglyphs
U+13430 ...	U+1345F	Egyptian Hieroglyph Format Controls
U+14400 ...	U+1467F	Anatolian Hieroglyphs
U+16800 ...	U+16A3F	Bamum Supplement
U+16A40 ...	U+16A6F	Mro
U+16A70 ...	U+16ACF	Tangsa
U+16AD0 ...	U+16AFF	Bassa Vah
U+16B00 ...	U+16B8F	Pahawh Hmong
U+16E40 ...	U+16E9F	Medefaidrin
U+16F00 ...	U+16F9F	Miao
U+16FE0 ...	U+16FFF	Ideographic Symbols and Punctuation
U+17000 ...	U+187FF	Tangut
U+18800 ...	U+18AFF	Tangut Components
U+18B00 ...	U+18CFF	Khitan Small Script
U+18D00 ...	U+18D7F	Tangut Supplement
U+1AFF0 ...	U+1AFFF	Kana Extended-B
U+1B000 ...	U+1B0FF	Kana Supplement
U+1B100 ...	U+1B12F	Kana Extended-A
U+1B130 ...	U+1B16F	Small Kana Extension
U+1B170 ...	U+1B2FF	Nushu
U+1BC00 ...	U+1BC9F	Duployan
U+1BCA0 ...	U+1BCAF	Shorthand Format Controls
U+1CF00 ...	U+1CFCF	Znamenny Musical Notation
U+1D000 ...	U+1D0FF	Byzantine Musical Symbols
U+1D100 ...	U+1D1FF	Musical Symbols
U+1D200 ...	U+1D24F	Ancient Greek Musical Notation
U+1D2C0 ...	U+1D2DF	Kaktovik Numerals
U+1D2E0 ...	U+1D2FF	Mayan Numerals
U+1D300 ...	U+1D35F	Tai Xuan Jing Symbols
U+1D360 ...	U+1D37F	Counting Rod Numerals
U+1D400 ...	U+1D7FF	Mathematical Alphanumeric Symbols
U+1D800 ...	U+1DAAF	Sutton SignWriting
U+1DF00 ...	U+1DFFF	Latin Extended-G
U+1E000 ...	U+1E02F	Glagolitic Supplement
U+1E030 ...	U+1E08F	Cyrillic Extended-D
U+1E100 ...	U+1E14F	Nyiakeng Puachue Hmong

U+1E290 ...	U+1E2BF	Toto
U+1E2C0 ...	U+1E2FF	Wancho
U+1E4D0 ...	U+1E4FF	Nag Mundari
U+1E7E0 ...	U+1E7FF	Ethiopic Extended-B
U+1E800 ...	U+1E8DF	Mende Kikakui
U+1E900 ...	U+1E95F	Adlam
U+1EC70 ...	U+1ECBF	Indic Siyaq Numbers
U+1ED00 ...	U+1ED4F	Ottoman Siyaq Numbers
U+1EE00 ...	U+1EEFF	Arabic Mathematical Alphabetic Symbols
U+1F000 ...	U+1F02F	Mahjong Tiles
U+1F030 ...	U+1F09F	Domino Tiles
U+1F0A0 ...	U+1F0FF	Playing Cards
U+1F100 ...	U+1F1FF	Enclosed Alphanumeric Supplement
U+1F200 ...	U+1F2FF	Enclosed Ideographic Supplement
U+1F300 ...	U+1F5FF	Miscellaneous Symbols and Pictographs
U+1F600 ...	U+1F64F	Emoticons
U+1F650 ...	U+1F67F	Ornamental Dingbats
U+1F680 ...	U+1F6FF	Transport and Map Symbols
U+1F700 ...	U+1F77F	Alchemical Symbols
U+1F780 ...	U+1F7FF	Geometric Shapes Extended
U+1F800 ...	U+1F8FF	Supplemental Arrows-C
U+1F900 ...	U+1F9FF	Supplemental Symbols and Pictographs
U+1FA00 ...	U+1FA6F	Chess Symbols
U+1FA70 ...	U+1FAFF	Symbols and Pictographs Extended-A
U+1FB00 ...	U+1FBFF	Symbols for Legacy Computing
U+20000 ...	U+2A6DF	CJK Unified Ideographs Extension B
U+2A700 ...	U+2B73F	CJK Unified Ideographs Extension C
U+2B740 ...	U+2B81F	CJK Unified Ideographs Extension D
U+2B820 ...	U+2CEAF	CJK Unified Ideographs Extension E
U+2CEB0 ...	U+2EBEF	CJK Unified Ideographs Extension F
U+2EBF0 ...	U+2EE5F	CJK Unified Ideographs Extension I
U+2F800 ...	U+2FA1F	CJK Compatibility Ideographs Supplement
U+30000 ...	U+3134F	CJK Unified Ideographs Extension G
U+31350 ...	U+323AF	CJK Unified Ideographs Extension H
U+E0000 ...	U+E007F	Tags
U+E0100 ...	U+E01EF	Variation Selectors Supplement
U+F0000 ...	U+FFFFF	Supplementary Private Use Area-A

```
U+100000 ... U+10FFFF   Supplementary Private Use Area-B
```

Unicode 13.0 Character Samples

Some samples of characters added in Unicode 13.0 are provided here for the purpose of demonstration or performing browser testing.

5 samples of characters added in Unicode 13.0 standard published in 2020 are listed below with their glyphs, code points, code names and code blocks. If you see nothing or something strange between brackets in "Glyph Browser" column, you know that your browser (and the operating system) does not support this character.

```
Glyph    Glyph     Code      Code
Browser  Expected  Point     Name
```

(#)   ☺   U+1F972 (SMILING FACE WITH TEAR)
         Code Block: Supplemental Symbols and Pictograph

(#)   𐿋   U+10FCB (CHORASMIAN NUMBER ONE HUNDRED)
         Code Block: Chorasmian

(#   𘬑   U+18B11 (A KHITAN SMALL SCRIPT CHARACTER)
         Code Block: Khitan Small Script

(#   🄏   U+1F10F (CIRCLED DOLLAR SIGN WITH OVERLAID BACKSLASH)
         Code Block: Enclosed Alphanumeric Supplement

(#   🦭   U+1F9AD (SEAL)
         Code Block: Supplemental Symbols and Pictographs

Unicode 8.0 Character Samples

Some samples of characters added in Unicode 8.0 are provided here for the purpose of demonstration or performing browser testing.

5 samples of characters added in Unicode 8.0 standard published in 2015 are listed below with their glyphs, code points, code names and code blocks. If you see nothing or something strange between brackets in "Glyph Browser" column, you know that your browser (and the operating system) does not support this character.

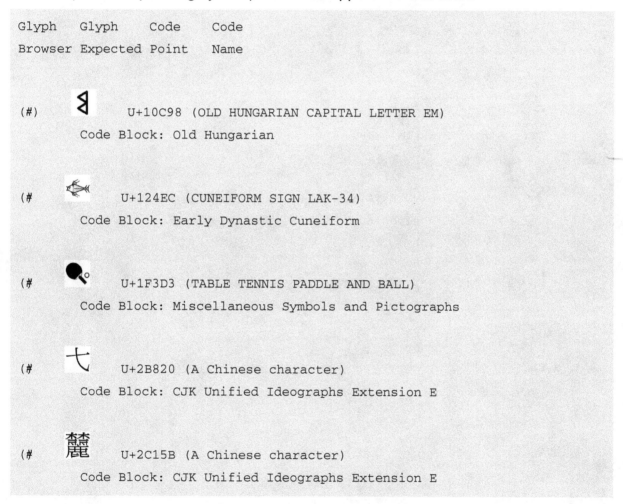

```
Glyph   Glyph    Code     Code
Browser Expected Point    Name


(#)        ᶌ          U+10C98 (OLD HUNGARIAN CAPITAL LETTER EM)
           Code Block: Old Hungarian


(#                    U+124EC (CUNEIFORM SIGN LAK-34)
           Code Block: Early Dynastic Cuneiform


(#                    U+1F3D3 (TABLE TENNIS PADDLE AND BALL)
           Code Block: Miscellaneous Symbols and Pictographs


(#         七         U+2B820 (A Chinese character)
           Code Block: CJK Unified Ideographs Extension E


(#         麤         U+2C15B (A Chinese character)
           Code Block: CJK Unified Ideographs Extension E
```

As of 2015, most Web browsers and PDF tools will not support any Unicode 8.0 characters.

Unicode 7.0 Character Samples

Some samples of characters added in Unicode 7.0 are provided here for the purpose of demonstration or performing browser testing.

5 samples of characters added in Unicode 7.0 standard published in 2014 are listed below with their glyphs, code points, code names and code blocks. If you see nothing or something strange between brackets in "Glyph Browser" column, you know that your browser (and the operating system) does not support this character.

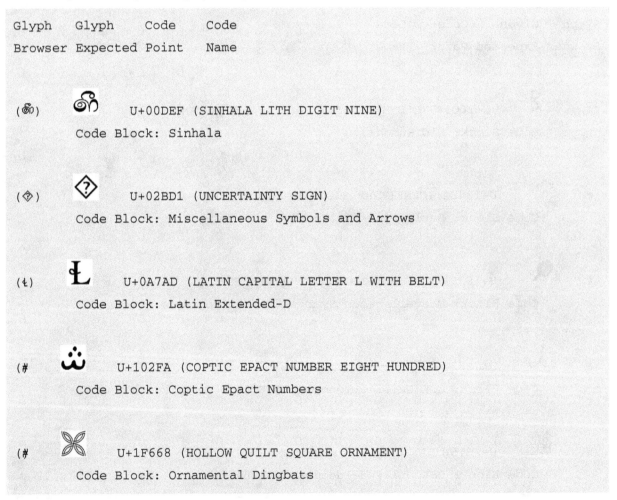

```
Glyph   Glyph    Code     Code
Browser Expected Point    Name

(෯)     ෯        U+0DEF (SINHALA LITH DIGIT NINE)
        Code Block: Sinhala

(⯑)     ⯑        U+02BD1 (UNCERTAINTY SIGN)
        Code Block: Miscellaneous Symbols and Arrows

(ɬ)     Ɬ        U+0A7AD (LATIN CAPITAL LETTER L WITH BELT)
        Code Block: Latin Extended-D

(#      𐋺        U+102FA (COPTIC EPACT NUMBER EIGHT HUNDRED)
        Code Block: Coptic Epact Numbers

(#      🙨        U+1F668 (HOLLOW QUILT SQUARE ORNAMENT)
        Code Block: Ornamental Dingbats
```

As of 2015, most Web browsers will not support any Unicode 7.0 characters.

But some PDF tools can use latest Unicode fonts to support some Unicode 7.0 characters.

Unicode 6.0 Character Samples

Some samples of characters added in Unicode 6.0 are provided here for the purpose of demonstration or performing browser testing.

5 samples of characters added in Unicode 6.0 standard published in 2011 are listed below with their glyphs, code points, code names and code blocks. If you see nothing or something strange between brackets in "Glyph Browser" column, you know that your browser (and the operating system) does not support this character.

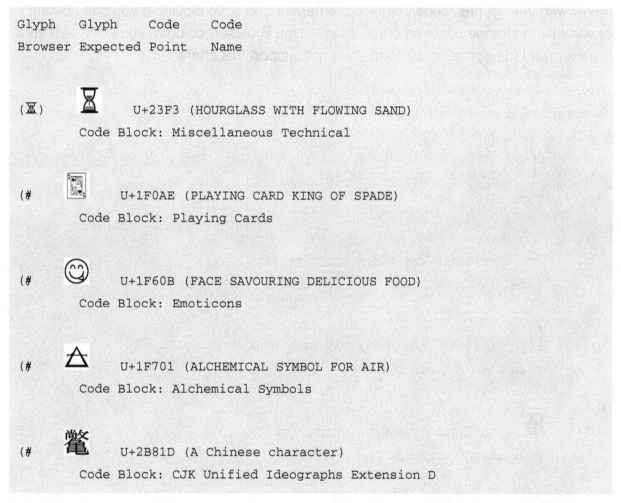

```
Glyph     Glyph       Code      Code
Browser   Expected    Point     Name


(⧖)         ⧖          U+23F3  (HOURGLASS WITH FLOWING SAND)
                    Code Block: Miscellaneous Technical


(#          🂮          U+1F0AE (PLAYING CARD KING OF SPADE)
                    Code Block: Playing Cards


(#          ☺          U+1F60B (FACE SAVOURING DELICIOUS FOOD)
                    Code Block: Emoticons


(#          🜁          U+1F701 (ALCHEMICAL SYMBOL FOR AIR)
                    Code Block: Alchemical Symbols


(#          鼇          U+2B81D (A Chinese character)
                    Code Block: CJK Unified Ideographs Extension D
```

My tests show that Windows 7 supports some Unicode 6.0 characters, like the HOURGLASS WITH FLOWING SAND character and FACE SAVOURING DELICIOUS FOOD character. But many other Unicode 6.0 characters are not supported.

Note that PDF generation tools may support different subsets of Unicode 6.0 characters, depending on which font files are used.

Unicode 5.0 Character Samples

Some samples of characters added in Unicode 5.0 are provided here for the purpose of demonstration or performing browser testing.

5 samples of characters added in Unicode 5.0 standard published in 2006 are listed below with their glyphs, code points, code names and code blocks. If you see nothing or something strange between brackets in "Glyph Browser" column, you know that your browser (and the operating system) does not support this character.

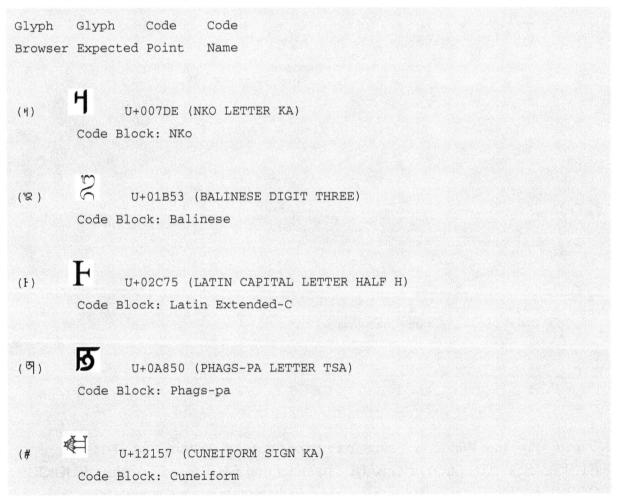

```
Glyph    Glyph      Code       Code
Browser  Expected   Point      Name


 (ꟼ)       Ꮋ          U+007DE  (NKO LETTER KA)
          Code Block: NKo


 (꛳ )       ꛓ         U+01B53  (BALINESE DIGIT THREE)
          Code Block: Balinese


 (Ⱶ)       Ⱶ         U+02C75  (LATIN CAPITAL LETTER HALF H)
          Code Block: Latin Extended-C


 (ꡅ)       ꡅ         U+0A850  (PHAGS-PA LETTER TSA)
          Code Block: Phags-pa


 (#        𒅗         U+12157  (CUNEIFORM SIGN KA)
          Code Block: Cuneiform
```

My tests show that Windows 7 is still not support some Unicode 5.0 characters, like the BALINESE DIGIT THREE character and the CUNEIFORM SIGN KA character 9 years after Unicode 5.0 was published.

Note that PDF generation tools may support different subsets of Unicode 5.0 characters, depending on which font files are used.

Unicode 4.0 Character Samples

Some samples of characters added in Unicode 4.0 are provided here for the purpose of demonstration or performing browser testing.

5 samples of characters added in Unicode 4.0 standard published in 2003 are listed below with their glyphs, code points, code names and code blocks. If you see nothing or something strange between brackets in "Glyph Browser" column, you know that your browser (and the operating system) does not support this character.

```
Glyph    Glyph     Code      Code
Browser  Expected  Point     Name


(‡)        ↕        U+02B0D (UP DOWN BLACK ARROW)
             Code Block: Miscellaneous Symbols and Arrows


(䷊)       ䷊        U+04DCA (HEXAGRAM FOR PEACE)
             Code Block: Yijing Hexagram Symbols


(#         𐂖        U+10096 (LINEAR B IDEOGRAM B131 WINE)
             Code Block: Linear B Ideograms


(#)        𐠬        U+1082C (CYPRIOT SYLLABLE SU)
             Code Block: Cypriot Syllabary


(#         𝌝        U+1D31D (TETRAGRAM FOR JOY)
```

```
Code Block: Tai Xuan Jing Symbols
```

My tests show that Windows 7 is still not support some Unicode 4.0 characters, like the LINEAR B IDEOGRAM B131 WINE character and the CYPRIOT SYLLABLE SU character 12 years after Unicode 4.0 was published.

Note that PDF generation tools may support different subsets of Unicode 4.0 characters, depending on which font files are used.

UTF-8 (Unicode Transformation Format - 8-Bit)

This chapter provides notes and tutorial examples on UTF-8 encoding. Topics including introduction of UTF-8 encoding; examples of encoded byte stream; UTF-8 encoding algorithm.

Conclusions:

- UTF-8 encoding is a variable-length 8-bit (1-byte) Unicode character encodings.

- UTF-8 is compatible with ASCII encoding. It is very efficient for Western language characters.

- UTF-8 is not so efficient for CJK (Chinese, Japanese and Korean) language characters, which are encoded into 3 bytes per character most of the time.

- The maximum number encoded bytes is 4 for characters in the latest version of Unicode character set - Unicode 5.0.

- "UTF-8, a transformation format of ISO 10646" at tools.ietf.org/html/rfc2279 gives official specifications of UTF-8 encoding.

UTF-8 Encoding

This section provides a quick introduction of the UTF-8 (Unicode Transformation Format - 8-bit) encoding for Unicode character set. It uses 1, 2, 3, or 4 bytes for each character.

UTF-8: A character encoding that maps code points of Unicode character set to a sequence of 1 byte (8 bits). UTF-8 stands for Unicode Transformation Format - 8-bit.

Here is my understanding of the UTF-8 specification. When UTF-8 encoding is used to encode (serialize) Unicode characters into a byte stream for communication or storage, the following logic should be used:

- If a code point is the U+0000...U+007F range, it can be viewed as a 7-bit integer, 0bxxxxxxx. Map the code point into 1 byte with the first high order bit set to 0 as: B1 = 0b0xxxxxx.

- If a code point is the U+0080...U+07FF range, it can be viewed as a 11-bit integer, 0byyyyyxxxxxx. Map the code point into 2 bytes with first 5 bits stored in the first byte and last 6 bits in the second byte: as: B1 = 0b110yyyyy, B2 = 0b10xxxxxx.

- If a code point is the U+0800...U+FFFF range, it can be viewed as a 16-bit integer, 0bzzzzyyyyyyxxxxxx. Map the code point into 3 bytes with first 4 bits stored in the first byte, next 6 bits in the second byte, and last 6 bits in the third byte: as: B1 = 0b1110zzzz, B2 = 0b10yyyyyy, B3 = 0b10xxxxxx.

- If a code point is the U+10000...U+10FFFF range, it can be viewed as a 21-bit integer, 0bvvvzzzzzzyyyyyyxxxxxx. Map the code point into 4 bytes with first 3 bits stored in the first byte, next 6 bits in the second byte, another 6 bits in the third byte, and last 6 bits in the fourth byte: as: B1 = 0b11110xxx, B2 = 0b10zzzzzz, B3 = 0b10yyyyyy, B4 = 0b10xxxxxx.

The above logic can also be summarized in a table like this:

```
                       Binary Format and Split Bytes
Code Point Range       Byte 1         Byte 2        Byte 3        Byte 4


U+000000...U+00007F    0bxxxxxxx
                       0b0xxxxxxx


U+000080...U+0007FF    0byyyyyxxxxxx
                       0b110yyyyy, 0b10xxxxxx


U+000800...U+00FFFF    0bzzzzyyyyyyxxxxxx
                       0b1110zzzz, 0b10yyyyyy, 0b10xxxxxx


U+010000...U+10FFFF    0bvvvzzzzzzyyyyyyxxxxxx
```

```
                    0b11110vvv, 0b10zzzzzz, 0b10yyyyyy, 0b10xxxxxx
```

For example, these 3 Unicode characters, U+004D, U+0061 and U+10000 will be converted into 0x4D61F0908080 when UTF-8 is used.

UTF-8 Encoding Algorithm

This section provides a tutorial example on how to write a programming algorithm to encode characters with UTF-8 encoding.

Here is an algorithm for UTF-8 encoding on a single character:

```
Input:
    unsigned integer c - the code point of the character to be encoded
Output:
    byte b1, b2, b3, b4 - the encoded sequence of bytes
Algorithm:
    if (c<0x80)
        b1 = c>>0  & 0x7F | 0x00
        b2 = null
        b3 = null
        b4 = null
    else if (c<0x0800)
        b1 = c>>6  & 0x1F | 0xC0
        b2 = c>>0  & 0x3F | 0x80
        b3 = null
        b4 = null
    else if (c<0x010000)
        b1 = c>>12 & 0x0F | 0xE0
        b2 = c>>6  & 0x3F | 0x80
        b3 = c>>0  & 0x3F | 0x80
        b4 = null
    else if (c<0x110000)
        b1 = c>>18 & 0x07 | 0xF0
        b2 = c>>12 & 0x3F | 0x80
        b3 = c>>6  & 0x3F | 0x80
```

```
      b4 = c>>0  & 0x3F | 0x80
  end if
```

Exercise: Write an algorithm to decode a UTF-8 encoded byte sequence.

Features of UTF-8 Encoding

This section provides a quick summary of features of UTF-8 encoding. UTF-8 is very efficient for Western language characters.

Features of UTF-8 encoding:

1.UTF-8 is very efficient in storage for characters in Western languages. The code points for most of characters in Western languages are in the U+0000...U+007F range, which will be encoded with 1 byte per character. The rest of characters will be encoded by two bytes. Some reports says that any text data in Western language will be encoded with 1.1 bytes per character on average. This is a big saving comparing with any other Unicode encodings.

2. UTF-8 is compatible with the single byte ASCII encoding. In another word, ASCII encoding can be viewed as a sub set of the UTF-8 encoding. Any ASCII byte stream is a valid UTF-8 byte stream.

3. UTF-8 is backward compatible with Unicode 3.0 character set, which only contains characters in the U+0000...U+FFFF range.

4. UTF-8 is less efficient in storage for characters in CJK (Chinese, Japanese, and Korean) languages comparing to UTF-16 encoding. The code points for most of characters in CJK languages are in the U+000800...U+00FFFF range, which will be encoded in UTF-8 with 3 bytes per character. UTF-16 will encode all characters 2 bytes per character.

5. Processing a UTF-8 encoded text files is relatively easy. If the leading bit of the first byte is a 0, then 1 byte is used to encoding this character. If the leading bit of the first byte is not a 0, then the number of non-zero leading bits is total number bytes used to encoding this character.

6. Another nice nature of UTF-8 encoding is that all subsequent bytes in encoded multi-byte sequence are having the pattern of 0b10xxxxxx in binary format. If you are looking

at one byte of an encoded character in the middle of the encoded stream, and want to find out the first byte of this encoded character, you just need to follow this simple logic:

```
while (current byte matches the bit pattern '10xxxxxx') {
    Current byte = previous byte
}
```

UTF-16, UTF-16BE and UTF-16LE Encodings

This chapter provides notes and tutorial examples on UTF-16, UTF-16BE and UTF-16LE encodings. Topics including encoding and decoding logics of UTF-16, UTF-16BE and UTF-16LE encodings; introduction of surrogate pairs; explanation of the use of BOM (Byte Order Mark).

Conclusions:

- UTF-16, UTF-16BE and UTF-16LE encodings are all variable-length 16-bit (2-byte) Unicode character encodings.

- Output byte streams of UTF-16 encoding may have 3 valid formats: Big-Endian without BOM, Big-Endian with BOM, and Little-Endian with BOM.

- UTF-16BE encoding is identical to the Big-Endian without BOM format of UTF-16 encoding.

- UTF-16LE encoding is identical to the Little-Endian with BOM format of UTF-16 encoding without using BOM.

- "UTF-16, an encoding of ISO 10646" at tools.ietf.org/html/rfc2781 gives official specifications of UTF-16, UTF-16BE and UTF-16LE encodings.

What Are Paired Surrogates

This section provides a quick introduction of paired surrogates which are pairs of 16-bit integers to represent Unicode code points in the U+10000...0x10FFFF range.

The goal UTF-16 encoding is to:

- Map Unicode code points in the range of U+0000...0xFFFF with 2 bytes (16 bits).

- Map Unicode code points in the range of U+10000...0x10FFFF with 4 bytes (32 bits).

The mapping for the U+0000...0xFFFF range is straightforward.

But the mapping for the U+10000...0x10FFFF range is tricky, because we want the resulting 4-byte stream can be recognized as 1 character in the U+10000...0x10FFFF range instead of 2 characters in the U+0000...0xFFFF range. This is achieved by using paired surrogates.

What Are Paired Surrogates? Paired surrogates are pairs of 2 16-bit unsigned integers in the surrogate area between 0xD800 and 0xDFFF. Since there are no Unicode characters assigned with code points in the surrogate area, Paired surrogates can be easily recognized as 1 character in the U+10000...0x10FFFF range.

The UTF-16 specification defines that the first surrogate must be in the high surrogate area between 0xD800 and 0xDBFF and the second surrogate in the low surrogate area between 0xDC00 and 0xDFFF.

Based on my understanding of the specification, here is the algorithm to convert a Unicode code point in the range of U+10000...0x10FFFF to a surrogate pair:

- Let U be the unsigned integer value of the give code point.

- Let U' = U - 0x10000. U' is less than or equal to 0xFFFFF and now can be expressed as an unassigned 20-bit integer.

- Divide 20 bits of U' into 2 blocks with 10 bits in each block as 0byyyyyyyyyyxxxxxxxxxx.

- Let S1 = 0xD800 + 0byyyyyyyyyy, or S1 = 0b110110yyyyyyyyyy. S1 is the first surrogate of the surrogate pair.

- Let S2 = 0xDC00 + 0bxxxxxxxxxx, or S2 = 0b110111xxxxxxxxxx. S2 is the second surrogate of the surrogate pair.

Exercise: Write an algorithm to convert a surrogate pair back to a Unicode code point.

UTF-16 Encoding

This section provides a quick introduction of the UTF-16 (Unicode Transformation Format - 16-bit) encoding for Unicode character set. Paired surrogates are used for characters in the U+10000...0x10FFFF range.

Once we learned how to convert Unicode code points in the U+10000...0x10FFFF range into paired surrogates, we are ready to learn how UTF-16 encoding works.

UTF-16: A character encoding that maps code points of Unicode character set to a sequence of 2 bytes (16 bits). UTF-16 stands for Unicode Transformation Format - 16-bit.

Here is my understanding of the UTF-16 specification. When UTF-16 encoding is used to encode (serialize) Unicode characters into a byte stream for communication or storage, there are 3 valid optional formats:

- Big-Endian without BOM Format - If the character is in the U+0000...0xFFFF range, convert the code point as an unassigned 16-bit integer into 2 bytes with the most significant byte first. If the character is in the U+10000...0x10FFFF range, convert the character into a surrogate pair, then convert each surrogate into 2 bytes with the most significant byte first.

- Big-Endian with BOM Format - Prepend 0xFEFF first. Then convert each character in the same way as the Big-Endian without BOM Format.

- Little-Endian with BOM Format - Prepend 0xFFFE first. Then convert each character in the same way as the Big-Endian without BOM Format except that 16-bit integers are converted into 2 bytes with the least significant byte first.

For example, all 3 encoding streams list below are valid UTF-16 encoded streams for 3 Unicode characters, U+004D, U+0061 and U+10000:

- Big-Endian Format - 0x004D0061D800DC00

- Big-Endian with BOM Format - 0xFEFF004D0061D800DC00

- Little-Endian with BOM Format - 0xFFFE4D00610000D800DC

When UTF-16 encoding is used to decode (deserialize) a byte stream into Unicode characters, the following logic should be used:

- Step 1 - Read the first 2 bytes.

- Step 2a - If the first 2 bytes is 0xFEFF, treat them as BOM (Byte Order Mark), and convert the rest of the byte stream in blocks of 2 bytes. Each block is converted to a 16-bit integer assuming the most significant byte first. Then process the converted integer stream according to Step 3a and 3b.

- Step 2b - If the first 2 bytes is 0xFFFE, treat them as BOM (Byte Order Mark), and convert the rest of the byte stream in blocks of 2 bytes. Each block is converted to a 16-bit integer assuming the least significant byte first. Then process the converted integer stream according to Step 3a and 3b.

- Step 2c - If the first 2 bytes is not 0xFEFF or 0xFFFE, convert the entire stream, including the first 2 bytes, in blocks of 2 bytes. Each block is converted to a 16-bit integer assuming the most significant byte first. Then process the converted integer stream according to Step 3a and 3b.

- Step 3a - If a converted integer is not in the surrogate area, i.e. < 0xD800 or > 0xDFFF, it represent the code point of the decode character.

- Step 3b - If a converted integer is in the surrogate area, i.e. >= 0xD800 and <= 0xDFFF, it represent the first surrogate of a surrogate pair. Take the next converted integer as the second surrogate and convert the surrogate pair to a Unicode character in the U+10000...0x10FFFF range.

UTF-16BE Encoding

This section provides a quick introduction of the UTF-16BE (Unicode Transformation Format - 16-bit Big Endian) encoding for Unicode character set. UTF-16BE is a variation of UTF-16.

UTF-16BE: A character encoding that maps code points of Unicode character set to a sequence of 2 bytes (16 bits). UTF-16BE stands for Unicode Transformation Format - 16-bit Big Endian.

Here is my understanding of the UTF-16BE specification. When UTF-16BE encoding is used to encode (serialize) Unicode characters into a byte stream for communication or storage, the resulting byte stream is identical to the Big-Endian without BOM Format of the UTF-16 encoding.

For example, these 3 Unicode characters, U+004D, U+0061 and U+10000 will be converted into 0x004D0061D800DC00 when UTF-16BE is used.

When UTF-16BE encoding is used to decode (deserialize) a byte stream into Unicode characters, the entire stream will be divided into blocks of 2 bytes. Each block is converted to a 16-bit integer assuming the most significant byte first. Then process the converted integer stream as described below:

- If a converted integer is not in the surrogate area, i.e. < 0xD800 or > 0xDFFF, it represent the code point of the decode character.

- If a converted integer is in the surrogate area, i.e. >= 0xD800 and <= 0xDFFF, it represent the first surrogate of a surrogate pair. Take the next converted integer as the second surrogate and convert the surrogate pair to a Unicode character in the U+10000...0x10FFFF range.

Note that the use of BOM (Byte Order Mark) is not part of the UTF-16BE specification. So you should:

- Not prepend BOM sequence, 0xFEFF, to the output byte stream when encoding.

- Not treat initial sequence of 0xFEFF as BOM when decoding. If it exists, convert the initial 0xFEFF sequence as a Unicode character, the ZERO WIDTH NO-BREAK SPACE, U+FEFF, character.

UTF-16LE Encoding

This section provides a quick introduction of the UTF-16LE (Unicode Transformation Format - 16-bit Little Endian) encoding for Unicode character set. UTF-16LE is a variation of UTF-16.

UTF-16LE: A character encoding that maps code points of Unicode character set to a sequence of 2 bytes (16 bits). UTF-16LE stands for Unicode Transformation Format - 16-bit Little Endian.

Here is my understanding of the UTF-16LE specification. When UTF-16LE encoding is used to encode (serialize) Unicode characters into a byte stream for communication or storage, the resulting byte stream is identical to the Little-Endian with BOM Format of the UTF-16 encoding except that BOM is not prepended to the byte stream.

For example, these 3 Unicode characters, U+004D, U+0061 and U+10000 will be converted into 0x4D00610000D800DC when UTF-16LE is used.

When UTF-16LE encoding is used to decode (deserialize) a byte stream into Unicode characters, the entire stream will be divided into blocks of 2 bytes. Each block is converted to a 16-bit integer assuming the least significant byte first. Then process the converted integer stream as described below:

- If a converted integer is not in the surrogate area, i.e. < 0xD800 or > 0xDFFF, it represent the code point of the decode character.

- If a converted integer is in the surrogate area, i.e. >= 0xD800 and <= 0xDFFF, it represent the first surrogate of a surrogate pair. Take the next converted integer as the second surrogate and convert the surrogate pair to a Unicode character in the U +10000...0x10FFFF range.

Note that the use of BOM (Byte Order Mark) is not part of the UTF-16LE specification. So you should:

- Not prepend BOM sequence, 0xFFFE, to the output byte stream when encoding.

- Not treat initial sequence of 0xFFFE as BOM when decoding. If it exists, convert the initial 0xFFFE sequence as a Unicode character, the ZERO WIDTH NO-BREAK SPACE, U+FEFF, character.

UTF-32, UTF-32BE and UTF-32LE Encodings

This chapter provides notes and tutorial examples on UTF-32, UTF-32BE and UTF-32LE encodings. Topics including encoding and decoding logics of UTF-32, UTF-32BE and UTF-32LE encodings; explanation of the use of BOM (Byte Order Mark).

Conclusions:

- UTF-32, UTF-32BE and UTF-32LE encodings are all fixed-length 32-bit (4-byte) Unicode character encodings.

- Output byte streams of UTF-32 encoding may have 3 valid formats: Big-Endian without BOM, Big-Endian with BOM, and Little-Endian with BOM.

- UTF-32BE encoding is identical to the Big-Endian without BOM format of UTF-32 encoding.

- UTF-32LE encoding is identical to the Little-Endian with BOM format of UTF-32 encoding without using BOM.

- "Unicode Standard Annex #19 - UTF-32" at unicode.org/reports/tr19/tr19-9.html gives quick and precise definitions of UTF-32, UTF-32BE and UTF-32LE encodings.

UTF-32 Encoding

This section provides a quick introduction of the UTF-32 (Unicode Transformation Format - 32-bit) encoding for Unicode character set. UTF-32 uses 32 bits or 4 bytes to encode each character.

UTF-32: A character encoding schema that maps code points of Unicode character set to a sequence of 4 bytes (32 bites). UTF-32 stands for Unicode Transformation Format - 32-bit.

Here is my understanding of the UTF-32 specification. When UTF-32 encoding is used to encode (serialize) Unicode characters into a byte stream for communication or storage, there are 3 valid optional formats:

- Big-Endian without BOM Format - Convert the code point of each character as a 32-bit integer into 4 bytes with the most significant byte first.

- Big-Endian with BOM Format - Prepend 0x0000FEFF, then convert the code point of each character as a 32-bit integer into 4 bytes with the most significant byte first.

- Little-Endian with BOM Format - Prepend 0xFFFE0000, then convert the code point of each character as a 32-bit integer into 4 bytes with the least significant byte first.

For example, all 3 encoding streams list below are valid UTF-32 encoded streams for 3 Unicode characters, U+004D, U+0061 and U+10000:

- Big-Endian Format - 0x0000004D0000006100010000>

- Big-Endian with BOM Format - 0x0000FEFF0000004D0000006100010000

- Little-Endian with BOM Format - 0xFFFE00004D000000610000000000100

When UTF-32 encoding is used to decode (deserialize) a byte stream into Unicode characters, the following logic should be used:

- Step 1 - Read the first 4 bytes.

- Step 2a - If the first 4 bytes is 0x0000FEFF, treat them as BOM (Byte Order Mark), and convert the rest of the byte stream in blocks of 4 bytes. Each block is converted to a 32-bit integer to represent a Unicode code point assuming the most significant byte first.

- Step 2b - If the first 4 bytes is 0xFFFE0000, treat them as BOM (Byte Order Mark), and convert the rest of the byte stream in blocks of 4 bytes. Each block is converted to a 32-bit integer to represent a Unicode code point assuming the least significant byte first.

- Step 2c - If the first 4 bytes is not 0x0000FEFF or 0xFFFE0000, convert the entire stream, including the first 4 bytes, in blocks of 4 bytes. Each block is converted to a

32-bit integer to represent a Unicode code point assuming the most significant byte first.

As of today, July 2009, there are not many applications that support UTF-32 encoding. I only see Firefox 3.0.11 on my Windows system that supports UTF-32 encoding.

UTF-32BE Encoding

This section provides a quick introduction of the UTF-32BE (Unicode Transformation Format - 32-bit Big Endian) encoding for Unicode character set.

UTF-32BE: A character encoding schema that maps code points of Unicode character set to a sequence of 4 bytes (32 bites). UTF-32BE stands for Unicode Transformation Format - 32-bit Big Endian.

Here is my understanding of the UTF-32BE specification. When UTF-32BE encoding is used to encode (serialize) Unicode characters into a byte stream for communication or storage, the code point of each character will be converted as a 32-bit integer into 4 bytes with the most significant byte first.

For example, these 3 Unicode characters, U+004D, U+0061 and U+10000 will be converted into 0x0000004D0000006100010000 when UTF-32BE is used.

When UTF-32BE encoding is used to decode (deserialize) a byte stream into Unicode characters, the entire stream will be divided into blocks of 4 bytes. Each block is converted to a 32-bit integer to represent a Unicode code point assuming the most significant byte first.

Note that the use of BOM (Byte Order Mark) is not part of the UTF-32BE specification. So you should:

- Not prepend BOM sequence, 0x0000FEFF, to the output byte stream when encoding.

- Not treat initial sequence of 0x0000FEFF as BOM when decoding. If it exists, convert the initial 0x0000FEFF sequence as a Unicode character, the ZERO WIDTH NO-BREAK SPACE, U+FEFF, character.

UTF-32LE Encoding

This section provides a quick introduction of the UTF-32LE (Unicode Transformation Format - 32-bit Big Endian) encoding for Unicode character set.

UTF-32LE: A character encoding schema that maps code points of Unicode character set to a sequence of 4 bytes (32 bites). UTF-32LE stands for Unicode Transformation Format - 32-bit Little Endian.

Here is my understanding of the UTF-32LE specification. When UTF-32LE encoding is used to encode (serialize) Unicode characters into a byte stream for communication or storage, the code point of each character will be converted as a 32-bit integer into 4 bytes with the least significant byte first.

For example, these 3 Unicode characters, U+004D, U+0061 and U+10000 will be converted into 0x4D0000006100000000000100 when UTF-32LE is used.

When UTF-32LE encoding is used to decode (deserialize) a byte stream into Unicode characters, the entire stream will be divided into blocks of 4 bytes. Each block is converted to a 32-bit integer to represent a Unicode code point assuming the least significant byte first.

Note that the use of BOM (Byte Order Mark) is not part of the UTF-32LE specification. So you should:

- Not prepend BOM sequence, 0xFFFE0000, to the output byte stream when encoding.

- Not treat initial sequence of 0xFFFE0000 as BOM when decoding. If it exists, convert the initial 0xFFFE0000 sequence as a Unicode character, the ZERO WIDTH NO-BREAK SPACE, U+FEFF. character.

Python Language and Unicode Characters

This chapter provides notes and tutorial examples on Unicode support in Python language. Topics including using 'str' data type to store single and multiple Unicode characters; Unicode escape sequences in 'str' literals; default Unicode encoding used in Python; str.encode() and bytes.decode() methods for encoding conversions; 'unicodedata' Module to retrieve Unicode properties.

Conclusions:

- Unicode is fully supported since Python 3.0.

- Default encoding for Python source code and conversion methods is UTF-8.

- "str" stores Unicode character strings as lists of Unicode code points.

- len(str) returns the number of Unicode code points, not the number of human language characters.

- \N{...}, \x.., \u...., and \U........ escape sequences in "str" literals can be used to specify Unicode code points.

- str.encode() converts character strings to byte sequences.

- bytes.decode() converts byte sequences to character strings.

- "unicodedata" module offers static methods to retrieve properties associated with code points defined by the Unicode standard.

Summary of Unicode Support in Python

This section provides a quick summary of Unicode support in Python language.

Unicode support in Python language can be summarized as below:

1. Full support of Unicode started in Python 3.0 - So if you are still using Python 2.x, you need to manage Unicode characters and code points in your own code.

2. Default encoding for Python source code is UTF-8 - This allows you to enter Unicode characters in your source code directly. If your Python script is stored in a non-UTF-8 encoding (e.g. latin-1, or gb2312), you need to add a special comment line to specify the encoding name like:

```
# -*- coding: latin-1 -*-
...
```

3. "str" data type stores Unicode characters as UTF-8 encoded bytes - The UTF-8 encoded bytes are internal storage structures with no public access.

4. Special escape sequences supported in "str" literals -

- Using the character name like "\N{GREEK CAPITAL LETTER DELTA}".

- Using a 8-bit hex value like "\xac", for code points that are small enough to be expressed in 2 hexsdecimal digits.

- Using a 16-bit hex value like "\u0394", for code points that are small enough to be expressed in 4 hexsdecimal digits.

- Using a 32-bit hex value like "\U00000394", for any code points.

5. chr(int) converts a code point to a character - A character is actually a "str" with 1 character.

6. ord(chat) converts a character to a code point

7. str.encode() converts "str" to "bytes" - It uses the default UTF-8 encoding or a given encoding.

8. bytes.decode() converts "bytes" to "str" - It uses the default UTF-8 encoding or a given encoding.

9. "unicodedata" module for Unicode properties - It provides a number of static methods to access varies properties of a given code point defined by the Unicode standard.

See next tutorials for examples demonstrating Unicode support in Python scripts.

Python Source Code Encoding

This section provides a tutorial example to demonstrate the default UTF-8 encoding of Python source code file and ways to change the default encoding.

When using Unicode characters in Python source code, you need to remember that:

- Python engine accepts Unicode characters in Python source code in UTF-8 encoding by default.

- Python engine scans for "coding: <encoding-name>" or "coding=<encoding-name>" in comment lines to change the default encoding.

Here is a Python script that generates 4 Python source code files for different encoding test:

```
# Source-Code-Encoding.py
# Copyright 2019 (c) HerongYang.com. All Rights Reserved.
#
import os

fd = os.open('Source-Code-Default.py', os.O_CREAT|os.O_WRONLY)
os.write(fd, b"print('Fran\xc3\xa7ais')")
os.close(fd)


fd = os.open('Source-Code-Latin-1.py', os.O_CREAT|os.O_WRONLY)
os.write(fd, b"# coding: latin-1\n")
os.write(fd, b"print('Fran\xe7ais')")
os.close(fd)


fd = os.open('Source-Code-Wrong-1.py', os.O_CREAT|os.O_WRONLY)
os.write(fd, b"print('Fran\xe7ais')")
```

```
os.close(fd)


fd = os.open('Source-Code-Wrong-2.py', os.O_CREAT|os.O_WRONLY)
os.write(fd, b"# coding=iso-8859-10\n")
os.write(fd, b"print('Fran\xe7ais')")
os.close(fd)
```

Run the above script, it will generate 4 Python source code files as shown below:

```
herong$ python3 --version
Python 3.8.0


herong$ python3 Source-Code-Encoding.py
herong$ ls -l
-rwxr-xr-x  1 herong   staff   18   Source-Code-Default.py
-rwxr-xr-x  1 herong   staff   35   Source-Code-Latin-1.py
-rwxr-xr-x  1 herong   staff   17   Source-Code-Wrong-1.py
-rwxr-xr-x  1 herong   staff   38   Source-Code-Wrong-2.py
```

Source-Code-Default.py uses the default source code encoding and contains a UTF 8 encoded character of \xc3\xa7. If you run it, you will see:

```
herong$ python3 Source-Code-Default.py


Français
```

Source-Code-Latin-1.py specifies the source encoding as "latin-1" and contains a Latin-1 encoded character of \xe7. If you run it, you will see the same result:

```
herong$ python3 Source-Code-Latin-1.py


Français
```

Source-Code-Wrong-2.py uses the default source code encoding and contains a Latin-1 encoded character of \xe7. If you run it, you will see an error message, because byte \xe7 is not compatible with UTF-8 encoding:

```
herong$ python3 Source-Code-Wrong-1.py


  File "Source-Code-Wrong-1.py", line 1
```

```
SyntaxError: Non-UTF-8 code starting with '\xe7' in file
Source-Code-Wrong-1.py on line 1, but no encoding declared;
see http://python.org/dev/peps/pep-0263/ for details
```

Source-Code-Wrong-1.py specifies the source encoding as "iso-8859-10" and contains a Latin-1 encoded character of \xe7. If you run it, you will see no errors. But it prints out a wrong character, because that byte \xe7 represents a different character in ISO-8859-10 than Latin-1:

```
herong$ python3 Source-Code-Wrong-2.py

Franḷais
```

Unicode Support on "str" Data Type

This section provides tutorial example on how to use the built-in data type 'str' to store Unicode characters as a list of code points.

When using Python built-in data type "str" to store Unicode characters, you need to remember that:

- "str" represents a Unicode character string as a list of Unicode code points.

- Each code point is stored as a byte sequence using the UTF-8 encoding.

- "str" literals in Python source code are decoded using the default UTF-8 encoding.

- "coding: <encoding-name>" or "coding=<encoding-name>" in comment lines can be used to change the source code default encoding.

- Escape sequence of "\N{<code_name>}" in "str" literal can be used to specify a Unicode code point by its name.

- Escape sequence of "\x.." in "str" literal can be used to specify a small Unicode code point by its 8-bit hexsdecimal value.

- Escape sequence of "\u...." in "str" literal can be used to specify a medium Unicode code point by its 16-bit hexsdecimal value.

- Escape sequence of "\U........" in "str" literal can be used to specify a large Unicode code point by its 32-bit hexsdecimal value.

- len(str) built-in function returns the number Unicode code points of a given Unicode character strings.

- The number of characters in a string may be less than the number of code points, because a single Unicode character may be represented with a combination of 2 code points.

- ord(char) built-in function returns the decimal value of the Unicode code point of a single character string.

- chr(int) built-in function returns a single character string represented by the given decimal value of a Unicode code point.

Here is a Python script that demonstrates how to use data type "str" to store Unicode character strings:

```
# str-Data-Type-on-Unicode.py
# Copyright 2019 (c) HerongYang.com. All Rights Reserved.
#
# "str" literals are decoded as UTF-8 encoded bytes by default
str = "Français"

# len(str) returns the number of code points in a "str"
num = len(str)

# a "str" can be accessed as a list of Unicode code points
for i in range(num):
  char = str[i]
  code = ord(char)
  print("{0} - {1}".format(hex(code), code))

# \N{}, \x, \u and \U escape sequences can be used in "str" literals
print("Français")
print("Fran\N{LATIN SMALL LETTER C WITH CEDILLA}ais")
print("Fran\xe7ais")
print("Fran\u00e7ais")
print("Fran\U000000e7ais")
```

```
# one character can be constructed with 2 combining code points
one = "\N{LATIN SMALL LETTER C WITH CEDILLA}"
two = "\N{LATIN SMALL LETTER C}\N{COMBINING CEDILLA}"
print("{0} with {1} code point".format(one, len(one)))
print("{0} with {1} code points".format(two, len(two)))
```

Run the above script, it will print the following output:

```
herong$ python3 str-Data-Type-on-Unicode.py

0x46 - 70
0x72 - 114
0x61 - 97
0x6e - 110
0xe7 - 231
0x61 - 97
0x69 - 105
0x73 - 115
Français
Français
Français
Français
Français
ç with 1 code points
ç with 2 code points
```

Unicode Character Encoding and Decoding

This section provides tutorial example on how to convert Unicode character strings to and from byte sequences based on different encoding standards using str.encode() and bytes.decode() methods.

Python support a large number of encodings that convert Unicode character strings into byte sequences according to different human language coding standards. Of course, Python allows you to convert those byte sequences back to Unicode characters strings.

str.encode(encoding='utf-8', errors='strict') - encode() is an instance method of a "str" object that converts the Unicode code points represented by the "str" object into a byte sequence according to the given encoding standard.

bytes.decode(encoding='utf-8', errors='strict') - decode() is an instance method of a "bytes" object that converts the byte sequence to a character string according to the given encoding standard.

Here are names of some encoding standards as described earlier in this book.

- "ascii" for the ASCII (American Standard Code for Information Interchange) encoding standard covering 128 characters including English letters and numbers.

- "latin-1" for the Latin-1, also called ISO 8859-1, standard covering 256 characters including letters for Western European languages.

- "gb2312" for the GB2312 standard covering basic Chinese characters.

- "utf-8" for the UTF-8 standard covering all Unicode characters.

- "utf-16" for the UTF-16 standard covering all Unicode characters.

- "utf-32" for the UTF-32 standard covering all Unicode characters.

Here is a Python script that shows you how to use str.encode() and bytes.decode() methods. The "replace" error handling option is used is used to avoid conversion exceptions.

```
# Character-Encoding-Decoding.py
# Copyright 2019 (c) HerongYang.com. All Rights Reserved.
#
en = "English"
fr = "Français"
zh = "中文"

print("Original character strings:")
print("  {0}, {1}, {2}".format(en, fr, zh))

print("Encoded with default UTF-8 encoding:")
enBin = en.encode()
frBin = fr.encode()
zhBin = zh.encode()
```

```
print("   {0}, {1}, {2}".format(enBin, frBin, zhBin))

print("Decoded back to Character strings:")
enStr = enBin.decode()
frStr = frBin.decode()
zhStr = zhBin.decode()
print("   {0}, {1}, {2}".format(enStr, frStr, zhStr))

print("Encoded and decoded back with Latin-1 encoding:")
enBin = en.encode("latin-1")
frBin = fr.encode("latin-1")
zhBin = zh.encode("latin-1", "replace")
enStr = enBin.decode("latin-1")
frStr = frBin.decode("latin-1")
zhStr = zhBin.decode("latin-1")
print("   {0}, {1}, {2}".format(enBin, frBin, zhBin))
print("   {0}, {1}, {2}".format(enStr, frStr, zhStr))

print("Encoded and decoded back with GB2312 encoding:")
enBin = en.encode("gb2312")
frBin = fr.encode("gb2312", "replace")
zhBin = zh.encode("gb2312")
enStr = enBin.decode("gb2312")
frStr = frBin.decode("gb2312")
zhStr = zhBin.decode("gb2312")
print("   {0}, {1}, {2}".format(enBin, frBin, zhBin))
print("   {0}, {1}, {2}".format(enStr, frStr, zhStr))
```

Run the above script, it will print the following output:

```
herong$ python3 Character-Encoding-Decoding.py

Original character strings:
    English, Français, 中文

Encoded with default UTF-8 encoding:
    b'English', b'Fran\xc3\xa7ais', b'\xe4\xb8\xad\xe6\x96\x87'
Decoded back to Character strings:
```

```
    English, Français, 中文

Encoded and decoded back with Latin-1 encoding:
    b'English', b'Fran\xe7ais', b'??'
    English, Français, ??

Encoded and decoded back with GB2312 encoding:
    b'English', b'Fran?ais', b'\xd6\xd0\xce\xc4'
    English, Fran?ais, 中文
```

The output confirms that Python does support encoding standards for different human languages. It has a large database that maps Unicode characters to codes defined in each individual encoding standard.

"unicodedata" Module for Unicode Properties

This section provides tutorial example on how to use the 'unicodedata' to retrieve properties of code points defined by the Unicode standard.

Python also offers a built-in module called "unicodedata" that provides a number of static methods to access varies properties of a given code point defined by the Unicode standard. Some commonly used "unicodedata" methods are given below:

unicodedata.unidata_version - Identifies the version number of the Unicode standard supported by the "unicodedata" module.

unicodedata.lookup(name) - Returns the code point as a "str" for a given Unicode character name.

unicodedata.name(char) - Returns the character name associated to a given Unicode code point.

unicodedata.category(char) - Returns the category code associated to a given Unicode code point.

unicodedata.combining(char) - Returns the combining class associated to a given Unicode code point.

unicodedata.decomposition(char) - Returns the decomposition string associated to a given Unicode code point.

unicodedata.normalize(form, str) - Converts a given string to the normalized form of a given form code, NFC (Normal Form Composition), NFKC (Normal Form Compatibility Composition), NFD (Normal Form Decomposition), or NFKD (Normal Form Compatibility Decomposition).

unicodedata.is_normalized(form, str) - Returns true if the given string is already normalized according to a given form code, NFC, NFKC, NFD, or NFKD.

unicodedata.decimal(char) - Returns the decimal value associated to a given Unicode code point.

unicodedata.digit(char) - Returns the digit value associated to a given Unicode code point.

unicodedata.numeric(char) - Returns the numeric value associated to a given Unicode code point.

Here is a Python script that shows you how to use the "unicodedata" module.

```
# unicodedata-Module-Test.py
# Copyright 2019 (c) HerongYang.com. All Rights Reserved.
#
import unicodedata

print("Unicode version: {0}".format(unicodedata.unidata_version))

char = unicodedata.lookup("Parenthesized Number Ten")
name = unicodedata.name(char)
print("{0} - {1}".format(char, name))
print("  category(): {0}".format(unicodedata.category(char)))
print("  combining(): {0}".format(unicodedata.combining(char)))
print("  decomposition(): {0}".format(unicodedata.decomposition(char)))
print("  decimal(): {0}".format(unicodedata.decimal(char, "N/A")))
print("  digit(): {0}".format(unicodedata.digit(char, "N/A")))
print("  numeric(): {0}".format(unicodedata.numeric(char, "N/A")))

char = unicodedata.lookup("Combining Cedilla")
name = unicodedata.name(char)
```

```
print("{0} - {1}".format(char, name))
print("   category(): {0}".format(unicodedata.category(char)))
print("   combining(): {0}".format(unicodedata.combining(char)))
print("   decomposition(): {0}".format(unicodedata.decomposition(char)))
print("   decimal(): {0}".format(unicodedata.decimal(char, "N/A")))
print("   digit(): {0}".format(unicodedata.digit(char, "N/A")))
print("   numeric(): {0}".format(unicodedata.numeric(char, "N/A")))


def normalized_info(form, str):
  norm = unicodedata.normalize(form, str)
  info = "normalize({0}, {1}): {2}, {3}, {4}".format(form, str, \
    norm, norm.encode(), len(norm))
  return info


char = unicodedata.lookup("Parenthesized Number Ten")
name = unicodedata.name(char)
print("{0} - {1}".format(char, name))
print("   {0}".format(normalized_info('NFC', char)))
print("   {0}".format(normalized_info('NFKC', char)))
print("   {0}".format(normalized_info('NFD', char)))
print("   {0}".format(normalized_info('NFKD', char)))


char = unicodedata.lookup("LATIN SMALL LETTER C WITH CEDILLA")
name = unicodedata.name(char)
print("{0} - {1}".format(char, name))
print("   {0}".format(normalized_info('NFC', char)))
print("   {0}".format(normalized_info('NFKC', char)))
print("   {0}".format(normalized_info('NFD', char)))
print("   {0}".format(normalized_info('NFKD', char)))
```

Run the above script, it will print the following output:

```
herong$ python3 unicodedata-Module-Test.py


Unicode version: 12.1.0


⑽ - PARENTHESIZED NUMBER TEN
  category(): No
```

```
combining(): 0

decomposition(): <compat> 0028 0031 0030 0029

decimal(): N/A

digit(): N/A

numeric(): 10.0


ؚ- COMBINING CEDILLA

category(): Mn

combining(): 202

decomposition():

decimal(): N/A

digit(): N/A

numeric(): N/A


⑽ - PARENTHESIZED NUMBER TEN

normalize(NFC, ⑽): ⑽, b'\xe2\x91\xbd', 1

normalize(NFKC, ⑽): (10), b'(10)', 4

normalize(NFD, ⑽): ⑽, b'\xe2\x91\xbd', 1

normalize(NFKD, ⑽): (10), b'(10)', 4


ç - LATIN SMALL LETTER C WITH CEDILLA

normalize(NFC, ç): ç, b'\xc3\xa7', 1

normalize(NFKC, ç): ç, b'\xc3\xa7', 1

normalize(NFD, ç): ç, b'c\xcc\xa7', 2

normalize(NFKD, ç): ç, b'c\xcc\xa7', 2
```

Java Language and Unicode Characters

This chapter provides notes and tutorial examples on Unicode support in Java language. Topics including Unicode versions supported in different JDK versions; using 'int' and 'String' data type to store single and multiple Unicode characters; Unicode utility methods in the 'Character' class; 'char' element index pointers and character locations in 'String' objects.

Conclusions:

- From JDK 1.0 to JDK 1.4, Java can only support BMP (Basic Multilingual Plane) characters.

- From J2SE 5.0 (JDK 1.5) to any newer versions, Java can support the full range, U+0000 to U+10FFFF, of Unicode characters.

- "Character" objects can not represent all Unicode characters any more. Store code points as "int" values represent Unicode characters.

- The "Character" class offers static utility methods to help Unicode character processing.

- The length() method on a "String" object returns the number of "char" elements used to store Unicode characters represented by the "String" object.

- The codePointCount() method on a "String" object returns the number of Unicode characters represented by the "String" object.

- The toCharArray() method on a "String" object returns the UTF-16BE encoded "char" sequence of Unicode characters represented by the "String" object.

- Non-ASCII characters can be represented as \uXXXX escape sequences follow the UTF-16 encoding rule in Java String literals.

- Non-ASCII characters can also be represented as UTF-8 encoding byte sequences follow the UTF-16 encoding rule in Java String literals. But the source code must be stored in UTF-8 encoding and compiled with the "-encoding UTF8" option.

Unicode Versions Supported in Java History

This section provides a quick summary of different Unicode versions supported in Java history. A major change was introduced in J2SE 5 to support Unicode 4.0 which contains supplementary characters in the range of U+10000 to U+10FFFF.

Unicode has been supported in the Java language since its first release in 1996. Both Unicode and Java have evolved with multiple versions and releases since then. Here is a summary of which version of Unicode is supported in which Java releases.

```
Java version    Release date        Unicode version
------------    ------------        ---------------
Java 15         March 2020          Unicode 13.0
Java 13         March 2019          Unicode 12.1
Java 11         March 2018          Unicode 10.0
Java 10         September 2018      Unicode 8.0
Java 9          September 2017      Unicode 8.0
Java 8          March 2014          Unicode 6.2
Java SE 7       July 28, 2011       Unicode 6.0
Java SE 6       December 11, 2006   Unicode 4.0
J2SE 5.0        September 30, 2004  Unicode 4.0
J2SE 1.4        February 6, 2002    Unicode 3.0
J2SE 1.3        May 8, 2000         Unicode 2.1
```

```
J2SE 1.2        December 8, 1998     Unicode 2.1
JDK 1.1         February 19, 1997    Unicode 2.0
JDK 1.1.7       September 12, 1997   Unicode 2.1
JDK 1.1         February 19, 1997    Unicode 2.0
JDK 1.0         January 23, 1996     Unicode 1.1.5
```

From JDK 1.0 to JDK 1.4, Java can only support Unicode code points in the range of U+0000 to U+FFFF. Unicode characters in this range are called BMP (Basic Multilingual Plane) characters.

Designers of JDK 1.0 used the following primitive types and built-in class types to support Unicode BMP characters in very natural way:

char - A primitive type with 16-bit storage size, which is perfected designed to store the code point value of a single BMP character.

Character - A built-in class that wraps a value of the primitive type char in an object. The Character class is perfectly designed to represent a single BMP character as an object. The Character class also provides some useful static methods for managing individual BMP characters.

String - A built-in class that wraps an array of primitive type char in an object. The String class is perfectly designed to represent a sequence of BMP characters as an object. The String class also provides some useful static and instance methods for managing a string of BMP characters.

Starting in J2SE 5.0, support of Unicode code points in the range of U+10000 to U+10FFFF was introduced in Java. Unicode characters in this range are called supplementary characters, implemented in Unicode 3.1 in 2001.

Designers of J2SE 5.0 did not introduce any new primitive types and built-in class types to support Unicode supplementary characters. What they did was:

• Use the existing primitive type **int** to represent a single supplementary character by storing its code point value as is.

• Use the existing primitive array type **char[]** to represent a sequence of supplementary characters by one surrogate char pair per supplementary character.

The surrogate char pair of a supplementary character is really the UTF-16BE encoded char sequence of the supplementary character. See other sections in this book for the UTF-16BE encoding algorithm.

Using UTF-16BE encoded char sequences to represent supplementary characters does give one main advantage to the existing class type **String**: A String object can still be viewed as a char sequence that represent a sequence of any Unicode characters: BMP characters and/or supplementary characters.

If you are interested in why J2SE 5.0 designers did not choose to add a new primitive type like char32 to help support supplementary characters, read the article "Supplementary Characters in the Java Platform" by Norbert Lindenberg and Masayoshi Okutsu at oracle.com/us/technologies/java/supplementary-142654.html.

'int' and 'String' - Basic Data Types for Unicode

This section provides an introduction on basic data types for storing Unicode characters in the full range of U+0000 to U+10FFFF: 'int' for a single Unicode character; 'String' for a sequence of Unicode characters.

As we learned from the previous section, the primitive type "char" is no longer capable to support Unicode characters in the full range of U+0000 to U+10FFFF. The best way to write Unicode-friendly Java applications with J2SE 5.0 or higher is to:

- Always use "int" primitive type to store a single Unicode character.

- Always use "String" class type to store a sequence of Unicode characters.

Other primitive types and class types can still be used to help managing Unicode characters, but you need to remember their risks and limitations:

- "byte" primitive type can only support ASCII characters in the range of U+0000 to U+00FF.

- "char" primitive type can only support BMP (Basic Multilingual Plane) characters in the range of U+0000 to U+FFFF.

- "Character" class type can only support BMP (Basic Multilingual Plane) characters in the range of U+0000 to U+FFFF.

- "char[]" array type should only be used to store UTF-16BE encoded "char" sequences of Unicode characters.

Examples of using Unicode-friendly data types:

```
int letterC = 0x43; // ASCII character
int degreeCelsius = 0x2103; // BMP character
int squaredC = 0x1F132; // Supplementary character

StringBuilder buffer = new StringBuilder();
buffer.appendCodePoint(letterC);
buffer.appendCodePoint(degreeCelsius);
buffer.appendCodePoint(squaredC);
String unicodeString = new String(buffer);
```

"Character" Class with Unicode Utility Methods

This section provides an introduction on 'Character' class static methods added since J2SE 5.0 as Unicode utility methods.

Since designers of J2SE 5.0 did not change the internal storage size for the "Character" class, it can not be used to support Unicode supplementary characters in the range of U+0000 to U+10FFFF. So you should avoid using "Character" class to represent a single Unicode character in the future to make your application Unicode-friendly.

However designers of J2SE 5.0 did add a number of static methods in the "Character" class as utility methods to help Unicode character processing. So take a look at some of them:

* static boolean isValidCodePoint(int codePoint) - Determines whether the specified code point is a valid Unicode code point value.

* static boolean isBmpCodePoint(int codePoint) - Determines whether the specified character (Unicode code point) is in the Basic Multilingual Plane (BMP). Such code points can be represented using a single char.

* static boolean isSupplementaryCodePoint(int codePoint) - Determines whether the specified character (Unicode code point) is in the supplementary character range.

* static int toCodePoint(char high, char low) - Converts the specified surrogate pair to its supplementary code point value. This method does not validate the specified surrogate pair. The caller must validate it using isSurrogatePair if necessary.

- static int codePointAt(char[] a, int index) - Returns the code point at the given index of the char array. If the char value at the given index in the char array is in the high-surrogate range, the following index is less than the length of the char array, and the char value at the following index is in the low-surrogate range, then the supplementary code point corresponding to this surrogate pair is returned. Otherwise, the char value at the given index is returned.

- static char highSurrogate(int codePoint) - Returns the leading surrogate (a high surrogate code unit) of the surrogate pair representing the specified supplementary character (Unicode code point) in the UTF-16 encoding. If the specified character is not a supplementary character, an unspecified char is returned.

- static char lowSurrogate(int codePoint) - Returns the trailing surrogate (a low surrogate code unit) of the surrogate pair representing the specified supplementary character (Unicode code point) in the UTF-16 encoding. If the specified character is not a supplementary character, an unspecified char is returned.

- static char[] toChars(int codePoint) - Converts the specified character (Unicode code point) to its UTF-16 representation stored in a char array. If the specified code point is a BMP (Basic Multilingual Plane or Plane 0) value, the resulting char array has the same value as codePoint. If the specified code point is a supplementary code point, the resulting char array has the corresponding surrogate pair.

- static boolean isDefined(int codePoint) - Determines if a character (Unicode code point) is defined in Unicode. A character is defined if at least one of the following is true: it has an entry in the UnicodeData file or it has a value in a range defined by the UnicodeData file.

- static String getName(int codePoint) - Returns the Unicode name of the specified character codePoint, or null if the code point is unassigned.

- static boolean isDigit(int codePoint) - Determines if the specified character (Unicode code point) is a digit. A character is a digit if its general category type, provided by getType(codePoint), is DECIMAL_DIGIT_NUMBER.

- static int getNumericValue(int codePoint) - Returns the int value that the specified character (Unicode code point) represents. For example, the character '\u216C' (the Roman numeral fifty) will return an int with a value of 50.

- static int getType(int codePoint) - Returns a value indicating a character's general category.

See the next section for a tutorial example on how to use "Character" class static methods.

Character.toChars() - "char" Sequence of Code Point

This section provides tutorial example on how to test 'Character' class toChars() static methods to convert Unicode code points to 'char' sequences, which is really identical to the byte sequences from the UTF-16BE encoding of the code point.

One interesting static method offered in the "Character" class is the "toChars(int codePoint)" method, which always returns "char" sequence for any given Unicode character. It returns 1 "char" if a BMP character is given; and 2 "char"s if a supplementary character is given.

Here is a tutorial example on how to use "toChars()" and other related methods:

```
/* UnicodeCharacterToChars.java
 * Copyright (c) 2019 HerongYang.com. All Rights Reserved.
 */
import java.io.*;
import java.nio.*;
import java.nio.charset.*;
class UnicodeCharacterToChars {
    static int[] unicodeList = {0x43, 0x2103, 0x1F132, 0x1F1A0,
        0x20FFFF};
    static char hexDigit[] = {'0', '1', '2', '3', '4', '5', '6', '7',
                              '8', '9', 'A', 'B', 'C', 'D', 'E', 'F'};
    public static void main(String[] arg) {
        try {
            for (int i=0; i<unicodeList.length; i++) {

// Starting with the code point value
                int codePoint  = unicodeList[i];

// Dumping data in HEX numbers
                System.out.print("\n");
                System.out.print("\n              Code point: "
```

```
                +intToHex(codePoint));


// Getting Unicode character basic properties
        System.out.print("\n              isDefined(): "
           +Character.isDefined(codePoint));
        System.out.print("\n                getName(): "
           +Character.getName(codePoint));
        System.out.print("\n           isBmpCodePoint(): "
           +Character.isBmpCodePoint(codePoint));
        System.out.print("\n isSupplementaryCodePoint(): "
           +Character.isSupplementaryCodePoint(codePoint));
        System.out.print("\n               charCount(): "
           +Character.charCount(codePoint));


// Getting surrogate char pair
        char charHigh = Character.highSurrogate(codePoint);
        char charLow = Character.lowSurrogate(codePoint);
        System.out.print("\n            highSurrogate(): "
           +charToHex(charHigh));
        System.out.print("\n             lowSurrogate(): "
           +charToHex(charLow));
        System.out.print("\n          isSurrogatePair(): "
           +Character.isSurrogatePair(charHigh, charLow));


// Getting char sequence
        char[] charSeq = Character.toChars(codePoint);
        System.out.print("\n                 toChars():");
        for (int j=0; j<charSeq.length; j++)
           System.out.print(" "+charToHex(charSeq[j]));


// Getting UTF-16BE byte sequence
        int[] intArray = {codePoint};
        String charString = new String(intArray, 0, 1);
        byte[] utf16Seq = charString.getBytes("UTF-16BE");
        System.out.print("\n    UTF-16BE byte sequence:");
        for (int j=0; j<utf16Seq.length; j++)
           System.out.print(" "+byteToHex(utf16Seq[j]));
```

```
         }
      } catch (Exception e) {
         System.out.print("\n"+e.toString());
      }
   }
   public static String byteToHex(byte b) {
      char[] a = { hexDigit[(b >> 4) & 0x0f], hexDigit[b & 0x0f] };
      return new String(a);
   }
   public static String charToHex(char c) {
      byte hi = (byte) (c >>> 8);
      byte lo = (byte) (c & 0xff);
      return byteToHex(hi) + byteToHex(lo);
   }
   public static String intToHex(int i) {
      char hi = (char) (i >>> 16);
      char lo = (char) (i & 0xffff);
      return charToHex(hi) + charToHex(lo);
   }
}
```

Compile and run it with Java 11:

```
C:\herong>javac UnicodeCharacterToChars.java

C:\herong>java UnicodeCharacterToChars

                 Code point: 00000043
                 isDefined(): true
                   getName(): LATIN CAPITAL LETTER C
           isBmpCodePoint(): true
 isSupplementaryCodePoint(): false
                  charCount(): 1
              highSurrogate(): D7C0
               lowSurrogate(): DC43
           isSurrogatePair(): false
                   toChars(): 0043
       UTF-16BE byte sequence: 00 43
```

```
              Code point: 00002103
              isDefined(): true
                getName(): DEGREE CELSIUS
          isBmpCodePoint(): true
isSupplementaryCodePoint(): false
               charCount(): 1
           highSurrogate(): D7C8
            lowSurrogate(): DD03
          isSurrogatePair(): false
                 toChars(): 2103
     UTF-16BE byte sequence: 21 03


              Code point: 0001F132
              isDefined(): true
                getName(): SQUARED LATIN CAPITAL LETTER C
          isBmpCodePoint(): false
isSupplementaryCodePoint(): true
               charCount(): 2
           highSurrogate(): D83C
            lowSurrogate(): DD32
          isSurrogatePair(): true
                 toChars(): D83C DD32
     UTF-16BE byte sequence: D8 3C DD 32


              Code point: 0001F1A0
              isDefined(): false
                getName(): null
          isBmpCodePoint(): false
isSupplementaryCodePoint(): true
               charCount(): 2
           highSurrogate(): D83C
            lowSurrogate(): DDA0
          isSurrogatePair(): true
                 toChars(): D83C DDA0
     UTF-16BE byte sequence: D8 3C DD A0
```

```
              Code point: 0020FFFF
              isDefined(): false
java.lang.IllegalArgumentException
```

The output confirms that:

- The isDefined(int codePoint) should be the first method to call make sure that the given int value represents a defined Unicode code point.

- If isDefined(int codePoint) returns false, stop calling other static methods. Calling Character method with an undefined code point value, may result exceptions.

- Java can return the character name for each defined Unicode character.

- For BMP characters, highSurrogate(int codePoint) and lowSurrogate(int codePoint) return invalid values.

- For supplementary characters, highSurrogate(int codePoint) and lowSurrogate(int codePoint) return a valid surrogate "char" pair.

- The toChars(int codePoint) also returns the surrogate "char" pair with high surrogate "char" first for supplementary characters.

- The "char" sequence returned by toChars(int codePoint) is identical to the byte sequence returned from the UTF-16BE encoding for both BMP and supplementary characters.

Character.getNumericValue() - Numeric Value of Code Point

This section provides tutorial example on how to test 'Character' class getNumericValue() static methods to obtain the numeric value associated with a given Unicode character.

One interesting static method offered in the "Character" class is the "getNumericValue(int codePoint)" method, which returns a numeric value represented by the given Unicode character.

Here is a tutorial example on how to use "getNumericValue()" and other related methods:

```
/* UnicodeCharacterNumeric.java
 * Copyright (c) 2019 HerongYang.com. All Rights Reserved.
 */
import java.io.*;
import java.nio.*;
import java.nio.charset.*;
class UnicodeCharacterNumeric {
   static int[] unicodeList = {0x37, 0x0667, 0x2166, 0x3286, 0x4E03,
      0x1F108};
   public static void main(String[] arg) {
      try {
         for (int i=0; i<unicodeList.length; i++) {

// Starting with the code point value
            int codePoint = unicodeList[i];

// Dumping data in HEX numbers
            System.out.print("\n");
            System.out.print("\n                      Code point: "
               +Integer.toHexString(codePoint).toUpperCase());

// Getting Unicode character numeric values
            System.out.print("\n                  isDefined(): "
               +Character.isDefined(codePoint));
            System.out.print("\n                    getName(): "
               +Character.getName(codePoint));
            System.out.print("\n            getNumericValue(): "
               +Character.getNumericValue(codePoint));

// Getting Unicode character type
            int intType = Character.getType(codePoint);
            System.out.print("\n                    getType(): "
               +intType);
            System.out.print("\n    is DECIMAL_DIGIT_NUMBER: "
               +(intType==Character.DECIMAL_DIGIT_NUMBER));
            System.out.print("\n                    isDigit(): "
               +Character.isDigit(codePoint));
```

```
      }
   } catch (Exception e) {
      System.out.print("\n"+e.toString());
   }
}
}
```

Compile and run it with Java 11:

```
C:\herong>javac UnicodeCharacterNumeric.java

C:\herong>java UnicodeCharacterNumeric

           Code point: 37
             getName(): DIGIT SEVEN
      getNumericValue(): 7
             getType(): 9
  is DECIMAL_DIGIT_NUMBER: true
             isDigit(): true


           Code point: 667
             getName(): ARABIC-INDIC DIGIT SEVEN
      getNumericValue(): 7
             getType(): 9
  is DECIMAL_DIGIT_NUMBER: true
             isDigit(): true


           Code point: 2166
             getName(): ROMAN NUMERAL SEVEN
      getNumericValue(): 7
             getType(): 10
  is DECIMAL_DIGIT_NUMBER: false
             isDigit(): false


           Code point: 3286
             getName(): CIRCLED IDEOGRAPH SEVEN
      getNumericValue(): 7
             getType(): 11
```

```
            is DECIMAL_DIGIT_NUMBER: false
                      isDigit(): false


                     Code point: 4E03
                       getName(): CJK UNIFIED IDEOGRAPHS 4E03
               getNumericValue(): -1
                       getType(): 5
            is DECIMAL_DIGIT_NUMBER: false
                      isDigit(): false


                     Code point: 1F108
                       getName(): DIGIT SEVEN COMMA
               getNumericValue(): 7
                       getType(): 11
            is DECIMAL_DIGIT_NUMBER: false
                      isDigit(): false
```

Some interesting notes on the output:

- Many Unicode characters that are not defined as digits, but they have numeric values. This is understandable. For example, "DIGIT SEVEN COMMA", 0x1F108, is not a digit. But it has a numeric value of 7. See the glyph of 0x1F108:

- It is strange to see that "ARABIC-INDIC DIGIT SEVEN", 0x0667, has numeric value of 7 and is defined as a digit! See the glyph of 0x0667:

- For some reason, the Chinese digit seven, 0x4E03, has no numeric value and is not defined as a digit! See the glyph of 0x4E03:

"String" Class with Unicode Utility Methods

This section provides an introduction on 'String' class methods added and modified since J2SE 5.0 to support Unicode character processing.

Since designers of J2SE 5.0 did not change the internal storage mechanism for the "String" class, Unicode supplementary characters will be stored as surrogate "char" pairs in "String" objects. In other words, a single supplementary character will take 2 storage positions in a "String" object. If all characters in a "String" object are supplementary characters, the length of the "String" object is 2 times of the number of characters.

If a "String" object contains both BMP characters and supplementary characters, there is no 1-to-1 relation between Unicode character positions and "char" storage positions. The n-th Unicode character may not be stored at the n-th or 2*n-th "char" position in a "String" object.

To help manage this inconvenience, designers of J2SE 5.0 enhanced some existing methods and added some new methods in the "String" class. Here are some examples:

- String(int[] codePoints, int offset, int count) constructor - Allocates a new String that contains characters from a subarray of the Unicode code point array argument. The offset argument is the index of the first code point of the subarray and the count argument specifies the length of the subarray. The contents of the subarray are converted to chars; subsequent modification of the int array does not affect the newly created string.

- String(char[] value) constructor - Allocates a new String so that it represents the sequence of characters currently contained in the character array argument. The contents of the character array are copied; subsequent modification of the character array does not affect the newly created string.

- int length() - Returns the length of this string. The length is equal to the number of Unicode code units in the string.

- char charAt(int index) - Returns the char value at the specified index. An index ranges from 0 to length() - 1. The first char value of the sequence is at index 0, the next at index 1, and so on, as for array indexing. If the char value specified by the index is a surrogate, the surrogate value is returned.

- int codePointAt(int index) - Returns the character (Unicode code point) at the specified index. The index refers to char values (Unicode code units) and ranges from 0 to length() - 1. If the char value specified at the given index is in the high-surrogate range, the following index is less than the length of this String, and the char value at the following index is in the low-surrogate range, then the supplementary code point corresponding to this surrogate pair is returned. Otherwise, the char value at the given index is returned.

- int codePointCount(int beginIndex, int endIndex) - Returns the number of Unicode code points in the specified text range of this String. The text range begins at the specified beginIndex and extends to the char at index endIndex - 1. Thus the length (in chars) of the text range is endIndex-beginIndex. Unpaired surrogates within the text range count as one code point each.

- byte[] getBytes(Charset charset) - Encodes this String into a sequence of bytes using the given charset, storing the result into a new byte array. This method always replaces malformed-input and unmappable-character sequences with this charset's default replacement byte array. The CharsetEncoder class should be used when more control over the encoding process is required.

- int indexOf(int ch) - Returns the index within this string of the first occurrence of the specified character. If a character with value ch occurs in the character sequence represented by this String object, then the index (in Unicode code units) of the first such occurrence is returned. For values of ch in the range from 0 to 0xFFFF (inclusive), this is the smallest value k such that: this.charAt(k) == ch, is true. For other values of ch, it is the smallest value k such that: this.codePointAt(k) == ch, is true. In either case, if no such character occurs in this string, then -1 is returned.

- String substring(int beginIndex, int endIndex) - Returns a new string that is a substring of this string. The substring begins at the specified beginIndex and extends to the character at index endIndex - 1. Thus the length of the substring is endIndex-beginIndex.

- char[] toCharArray() - Converts this string to a new character array.

- static String valueOf(char[] data) - Returns the string representation of the char array argument. The contents of the character array are copied; subsequent modification of the character array does not affect the newly created string.

String.length() Is Not Number of Characters

This section provides tutorial example on showing the difference between length() and codePointCount() methods. The difference between charAt(int index) and codePointAt(int index) is also demonstrated.

Because Unicode characters are stored in "String" objects as a mixed of single "char" elements and surrogate "char" element pairs, the "char" element index and Unicode character location are difficult to calculate.

Here is a tutorial example to show you this problem:

```
/* UnicodeStringIndex.java
 * Copyright (c) 2019 HerongYang.com. All Rights Reserved.
 */
import java.io.*;
class UnicodeStringIndex {
   static int[] unicodeList = {0x43, 0x2103, 0x1F132, 0x1F1A0,
      0x37, 0x0667, 0x2166, 0x3286, 0x4E03, 0x1F108};
   public static void main(String[] arg) {
      try {

// Constructing a String from a list of code points
         int num = unicodeList.length;
         String str = new String(unicodeList, 0, num);

// String length and code point count
         System.out.print("\n # of Unicode characters: "+num);
         System.out.print("\n        codePointCount(): "
            +str.codePointCount(0,str.length()));
         System.out.print("\n                 length(): "
            +str.length());

// String element at a BMP position
         System.out.print("\n              charAt(1): "
            +Integer.toHexString(str.charAt(1)));
         System.out.print("\n           codePointAt(1): "
            +Integer.toHexString(str.codePointAt(1)));

// String element at a high surrogate position
         char high = str.charAt(2);
         System.out.print("\n              charAt(2): "
            +Integer.toHexString(high));
         System.out.print("\n           codePointAt(2): "
            +Integer.toHexString(str.codePointAt(2)));

// String element at a low surrogate position
         char low = str.charAt(3);
         System.out.print("\n              charAt(3): "
```

```
            +Integer.toHexString(low));
        System.out.print("\n            codePointAt(3): "
            +Integer.toHexString(str.codePointAt(3)));


// validating the surrogate char pair
        int code = Character.toCodePoint(high, low);
        System.out.print("\n Character.toCodePoint(): "
            +Integer.toHexString(Character.toCodePoint(high, low)));
    } catch (Exception e) {
        System.out.print("\n"+e.toString());
    }
  }
}
```

Compile and run it with Java 11:

```
C:\herong>javac UnicodeStringIndex.java

C:\herong>java UnicodeStringIndex
 # of Unicode characters: 10
        codePointCount(): 10
                length(): 13
                charAt(1): 2103
            codePointAt(1): 2103
                charAt(2): d83c
            codePointAt(2): 1f132
                charAt(3): dd32
            codePointAt(3): dd32
 Character.toCodePoint(): 1f132
```

The output confirms that:

- codePointCount() returns the number Unicode characters in the "String" object.

- length() returns the number of "char" elements in the "String" object. length() is always greater than or equal to codePointCount().

- charAt() always return the "char" value at the given "char" index. It returns the high surrogate "char", if the given index points to the first "char" of a supplementary character - see charAt(2) in the output. It returns the low surrogate "char", if the given index points to the second "char" of a supplementary character - see charAt(3) in the output.

- codePointAt() returns the correct code point value, if the given index points to a BMP character - see codePointAt(1). It returns the correct code point value, if the given index points to the first "char" of a supplementary character. - see codePointAt(2). It returns the low surrogate "char", if the given index points to the second "char" of a supplementary character. - see codePointAt(3).

String.toCharArray() Returns the UTF-16BE Sequence

This section provides tutorial example on showing that the output of toCharArray() is the same as getBytes('UTF-16BE') at the bit level.

Another way to look at a "String" object is to dump it into a "char" sequence or a "byte" sequence with different encoding algorithms:

```
/* UnicodeStringEncoding.java
 * Copyright (c) 2019 HerongYang.com. All Rights Reserved.
 */
import java.io.*;
class UnicodeStringEncoding {
    static int[] unicodeList = {0x43, 0x2103, 0x1F132, 0x1F1A0};
    static char hexDigit[] = {'0', '1', '2', '3', '4', '5', '6', '7',
                              '8', '9', 'A', 'B', 'C', 'D', 'E', 'F'};
    public static void main(String[] arg) {
        try {

// Constructing a String from a list of code points
        int num = unicodeList.length;
        String str = new String(unicodeList, 0, num);

// String length and code point count
        System.out.print("\n # of Unicode characters: "+num);
        System.out.print("\n          codePointCount(): "
            +str.codePointCount(0,str.length()));
        System.out.print("\n                  length(): "
```

```
                +str.length());

// Getting the char sequence
        char[] charSeq = str.toCharArray();
        System.out.print("\n             toCharArray():");
        printChars(charSeq);

// Getting Unicode encoding sequences
        byte[] byteSeq8 = str.getBytes("UTF-8");
        System.out.print("\n          getBytes(UTF-8):");
        printBytes(byteSeq8);
        byte[] byteSeq16 = str.getBytes("UTF-16BE");
        System.out.print("\n       getBytes(UTF-16BE):");
        printBytes(byteSeq16);
        byte[] byteSeq32 = str.getBytes("UTF-32BE");
        System.out.print("\n       getBytes(UTF-32BE):");
        printBytes(byteSeq32);
    } catch (Exception e) {
        System.out.print("\n"+e.toString());
    }
}
public static void printBytes(byte[] b) {
    for (int j=0; j<b.length; j++)
        System.out.print(" "+byteToHex(b[j]));
}
public static String byteToHex(byte b) {
    char[] a = { hexDigit[(b >> 4) & 0x0f], hexDigit[b & 0x0f] };
    return new String(a);
}
public static void printChars(char[] c) {
    for (int j=0; j<c.length; j++)
        System.out.print(" "+charToHex(c[j]));
}
public static String charToHex(char c) {
    byte hi = (byte) (c >>> 8);
    byte lo = (byte) (c & 0xff);
    return byteToHex(hi) + byteToHex(lo);
```

```
    }
}
```

Compile and run it with Java 11:

```
C:\herong>javac UnicodeStringEncoding.java

C:\herong>java UnicodeStringEncoding
 # of Unicode characters: 4
       codePointCount(): 4
               length(): 6
           toCharArray(): 0043 2103 D83C DD32 D83C DDA0
        getBytes(UTF-8): 43 E2 84 83 F0 9F 84 B2 F0 9F 86 A0
     getBytes(UTF-16BE): 00 43 21 03 D8 3C DD 32 D8 3C DD A0
     getBytes(UTF-32BE): 00 00 00 43 00 00 21 03 00 01 F1 32 00 01...
```

The output confirms that:

- toCharArray() returns the same output as the getByte("UTF-16BE") at the bit level. In other words, Unicode characters are stored in a "String" object as a UTF-16BE encoded "char" sequence.

- getByte("UTF-16BE") returns the same output as the original code point value list at the bit level.

String Literals and Source Code Encoding

This section provides tutorial example on how to represent non-ASCII characters in UTF-8 encoding byte sequences as part of String literals in the Java source code.

In previous tutorials, we have learned how to represent non-ASCII characters in \uXXXX escape sequences as part of String literals in Java source code.

In this tutorial, we will learn how to represent non-ASCII characters in UTF-8 encoding byte sequences as part of String literals in Java source code.

Here is our test string that contains 2 Non-ASCII characters:

```
Delicious food U+1F60B takes time U+23F3
```

```
Where:
    U+1F60B: FACE SAVOURING DELICIOUS FOOD
    U+23F3: HOURGLASS WITH FLOWING SAND
```

Our test string should be displayed like this, if you have the correct Unicode font installed on your computer.

```
Delicious food 😊 takes time ⌛
```

In our first test program, we will continue to use \uXXXX sequences in our source code. Note that U+1F60B character needs to be encoded as a surrogate pair of \uD83D \uDE0B based on the UTF-16 encoding rule.

```java
/* UnicodeStringLiterals.java
 * Copyright (c) 2019 HerongYang.com. All Rights Reserved.
 */
class UnicodeStringLiterals {
   public static void main(String[] arg) {
      try {
         String str = "Delicious food \uD83D\uDE0B takes time \u23F3";
         System.out.print("\ncodePointCount(): "
            +str.codePointCount(0,str.length()));
         System.out.print("\n          length(): "
            +str.length());
         System.out.print("\n      String dump: ");
         printString(str);
      } catch (Exception e) {
         System.out.print("\n"+e.toString());
      }
   }
   public static void printString(String s) {
      char[] chars = s.toCharArray();
      for (char c : chars) {
         byte hi = (byte) (c >>> 8);
         byte lo = (byte) (c & 0xff);
         System.out.print(String.format("%02X%02X ", hi, lo));
      }
   }
```

```
    }
}
```

Compile and run it with Java 11:

```
C:\herong>javac UnicodeStringLiterals.java

C:\herong>java UnicodeStringLiterals
codePointCount(): 29
        length(): 30
     String dump: 0044 0065 006C 0069 0063 0069 006F 0075 0073 0020
                  0066 006F 006F 0064 0020 D83D DE0B 0020 0074 0061
                  006B 0065 0073 0020 0074 0069 006D 0065 0020 23F3
```

In our second test program, we will continue to use UTF-8 encoding byte sequences in our source code. This program is definitely better than the first program, because you can actually see non-ASCII characters displayed in the source code.

```
/* UnicodeStringLiteralsUTF8.java
 * Copyright (c) 2019 HerongYang.com. All Rights Reserved.
 */
import java.io.*;
class UnicodeStringLiteralsUTF8 {
   public static void main(String[] arg) {
      try {
         String str = "Delicious food #takes time ⏳";
         System.out.print("\ncodePointCount(): "
            +str.codePointCount(0,str.length()));
         System.out.print("\n        length(): "
            +str.length());
         System.out.print("\n     String dump: ");
         printString(str);
      } catch (Exception e) {
         System.out.print("\n"+e.toString());
      }
   }
   public static void printString(String s) {
      char[] chars = s.toCharArray();
      for (char c : chars) {
```

```
        byte hi = (byte) (c >>> 8);
        byte lo = (byte) (c & 0xff);
        System.out.print(String.format("%02X%02X ", hi, lo));
      }
   }
}
```

This time, we need to make sure that UnicodeStringLiteralsUTF8.java is saved as a
UTF-8 encoding file and compile with the "-encoding UTF8" option:

```
C:\herong>javac -encoding UTF8 UnicodeStringLiteralsUTF8.java

C:\herong>java UnicodeStringLiteralsUTF8
codePointCount(): 29
        length(): 30
    String dump: 0044 0065 006C 0069 0063 0069 006F 0075 0073 0020
                 0066 006F 006F 0064 0020 D83D DE0B 0020 0074 0061
                 006B 0065 0073 0020 0074 0069 006D 0065 0020 23F3
```

The output is identical to the first program. This proves that we have properly
represented non-ASCII characters in UTF-8 encoding byte sequences as part of String
literals in the Java source code.

Character Encoding in Java

This chapter provides notes and tutorial examples on character encoding in Java. Topics including supported encodings in Java SE 7; using encoding and decoding methods; examples of encoded byte sequences of various encodings.

Conclusions:

- As of Java 11, Java supports Unicode version 10.0.

- 171 encodings are supported in Java 11.

- Java 11 offers 4 ways to encode and decode characters with any supported encoding.

What Is Character Encoding

This section provides a quick introduction of Unicode character encodings and other local language encodings that are supported by Java.

Character Encoding: A map scheme between code points of a coded character set and sequences of bytes.

Coded Character Set: A character set in which each character has an assigned integral number.

Code Point: An integral number assigned to a character in a coded character set. As of Unicode 6.1, introduced in January, 2012, Unicode code point values have a range from 0x0000 to 0x10FFFF.

Unicode: A coded character set that contains all characters used in the written languages of the world and special symbols. As as Unicode 6.1, introduced in January, 2012, Unicode character set contains 110,181 characters.

The standard Unicode encoding is called UTF-32BE (Unicode Transformation Format - 32-bit Big Endian), which maps every Unicode character to a sequence of 4 bytes. For any given Unicode character, the UTF-32BE encoded byte sequence can be obtained by putting the character's code point integer number in the 4-byte binary format with the most significant byte listed first.

There are also other character encodings used on the Unicode character set, as described in previous chapters:

- UTF-32BE - The standard Unicode character encoding as mentioned above.

- UTF-32LE - Same as UTF-32BE, except that the least significant byte is listed first.

- UTF-16BE - Every Unicode character is mapped to a sequence of 2 or 4 bytes with the most significant byte listed first.

- UTF-16LE - Same as UTF-16BE, except that the least significant byte is listed first.

- UTF-8 - Every Unicode character is mapped to a sequence of 1, 2, 3 or 4 byte.

Since Unicode character set is a super set of many local language character sets, many other character encodings can also be applied to different subsets of the Unicode character set. Here are some examples of local language character encodings:

- ASCII - The standard encoding for the ASCII character set.

- ISO-8859-1 - The ISO standard encoding for Latin character set.

- GBK - A standard encoding for simplified Chinese character set.

- Big5 - A standard encoding for traditional Chinese character set.

As of Java 11, released in July 2011, Java language can support the Unicode character set defined in Unicode 10.0. UTF-32, UTF-16, and UTF-8 encodings are fully supported in Java.

Java can also help to you to perform local language character encodings too. See the next tutorial for full list of encodings supported in Java 11.

Java offers the following built-in classes to support Unicode character set, local language character subsets, and their encodings:

- java.nio.charset.Charset - Defined in the JDK document as "A named mapping between sequences of sixteen-bit Unicode code units and sequences of bytes. This class defines methods for creating decoders and encoders and for retrieving the various names associated with a charset. Instances of this class are immutable." The "Charset" class represents a particular character encoding defined a particular character set.

- java.nio.charset.CharsetEncoder - Defined in the JDK document as "An engine that can transform a sequence of sixteen-bit Unicode characters into a sequence of bytes in a specific charset."

- java.nio.charset.CharsetDecoder - Defined in the JDK document as "An engine that can transform a sequence of bytes in a specific charset into a sequence of sixteen-bit Unicode characters."

List of Supported Character Encodings in Java

This section provides a list of supported character encodings supported in Java. The list is generated using the availableCharsets() static method in the java.nio.charset.Charset class.

Before looking at how to perform an character encoding, let's see how many encodings are supported in Java 11 using the availableCharsets() static method in the java.nio.charset.Charset class.

Here is my tutorial program to display all the supported character encodings in Java:

```
/* Encodings.java
 * Copyright (c) 2019 HerongYang.com. All Rights Reserved.
 */
```

```
import java.nio.charset.*;
import java.util.*;
class Encodings {
   public static void main(String[] arg) {
      SortedMap m = Charset.availableCharsets();
      Set k = m.keySet();
      System.out.println("Canonical name, Display name,"
         +" Can encode, Aliases");
      Iterator i = k.iterator();
      while (i.hasNext()) {
         String n = (String) i.next();
         Charset e = (Charset) m.get(n);
         String d = e.displayName();
         boolean c = e.canEncode();
         System.out.print(n+", "+d+", "+c);
         Set s = e.aliases();
         Iterator j = s.iterator();
         while (j.hasNext()) {
            String a = (String) j.next();
            System.out.print(", "+a);
         }
         System.out.println("");
      }
   }
}
```

Compile and run it with Java 11:

```
C:\herong>javac Encodings.java


C:\herong>java Encodings
Canonical name, Display name, Can encode, Aliases
Big5, Big5, true, csBig5
Big5-HKSCS, Big5-HKSCS, true, big5-hkscs, big5hk, Big5_HKSCS, big5hkscs
CESU-8, CESU-8, true, CESU8, csCESU-8
EUC-JP, EUC-JP, true, csEUCPkdFmtjapanese, x-euc-jp, eucjis, Extended_...
EUC-KR, EUC-KR, true, ksc5601-1987, csEUCKR, ksc5601_1987, ksc5601, ...
GB18030, GB18030, true, gb18030-2000
```

```
GB2312, GB2312, true, gb2312, euc-cn, x-EUC-CN, euccn, EUC_CN, gb2312-...
GBK, GBK, true, CP936, windows-936
IBM-Thai, IBM-Thai, true, ibm-838, ibm838, 838, cp838
IBM00858, IBM00858, true, cp858, 858, PC-Multilingual-850+euro, ...
IBM01140, IBM01140, true, cp1140, 1140, cp01140, ebcdic-us-037+euro, ...
IBM01141, IBM01141, true, 1141, cp1141, cp01141, ccsid01141, ebcdic-...
IBM01142, IBM01142, true, 1142, cp1142, cp01142, ccsid01142, ebcdic-...
IBM01143, IBM01143, true, 1143, cp01143, ccsid01143, cp1143, ebcdic-...
IBM01144, IBM01144, true, cp01144, ccsid01144, ebcdic-it-280+euro, ...
IBM01145, IBM01145, true, ccsid01145, ebcdic-es-284+euro, 1145, cp1145,...
IBM01146, IBM01146, true, ebcdic-gb-285+euro, 1146, cp1146, cp01146, ...
IBM01147, IBM01147, true, cp1147, 1147, cp01147, ccsid01147, ebcdic-fr-...
IBM01148, IBM01148, true, cp1148, ebcdic-international-500+euro, 1148, ...
IBM01149, IBM01149, true, ebcdic-s-871+euro, 1149, cp1149, cp01149, ...
IBM037, IBM037, true, cp037, ibm037, ibm-037, csIBM037, ebcdic-cp-us, ...
IBM1026, IBM1026, true, cp1026, ibm-1026, 1026, ibm1026
IBM1047, IBM1047, true, ibm-1047, 1047, cp1047
IBM273, IBM273, true, ibm-273, ibm273, 273, cp273
IBM277, IBM277, true, ibm277, 277, cp277, ibm-277
IBM278, IBM278, true, cp278, 278, ibm-278, ebcdic-cp-se, csIBM278, ...
IBM280, IBM280, true, ibm280, 280, cp280, ibm-280
IBM284, IBM284, true, csIBM284, ibm-284, cpibm284, ibm284, 284, ...
IBM285, IBM285, true, csIBM285, cp285, ebcdic-gb, ibm-285, cpibm285, ...
IBM290, IBM290, true, ibm290, 290, cp290, EBCDIC-JP-kana, csIBM290, ...
IBM297, IBM297, true, 297, csIBM297, cp297, ibm297, ibm-297, ...
IBM420, IBM420, true, ibm420, 420, cp420, csIBM420, ibm-420, ...
IBM424, IBM424, true, ebcdic-cp-he, csIBM424, ibm-424, ibm424, 424, ...
IBM437, IBM437, true, ibm437, 437, ibm-437, cspc8codepage437, cp437, ...
IBM500, IBM500, true, ibm-500, ibm500, 500, ebcdic-cp-bh, ...
IBM775, IBM775, true, ibm-775, ibm775, 775, cp775
IBM850, IBM850, true, cp850, cspc850multilingual, ibm850, 850, ibm-850
IBM852, IBM852, true, csPCp852, ibm-852, ibm852, 852, cp852
IBM855, IBM855, true, ibm855, 855, ibm-855, cp855, cspcp855
IBM857, IBM857, true, ibm857, 857, cp857, csIBM857, ibm-857
IBM860, IBM860, true, ibm860, 860, cp860, csIBM860, ibm-860
IBM861, IBM861, true, cp861, ibm861, 861, ibm-861, cp-is, csIBM861
IBM862, IBM862, true, csIBM862, cp862, ibm862, 862, cspc862latinhebrew,...
```

```
IBM863, IBM863, true, csIBM863, ibm-863, ibm863, 863, cp863
IBM864, IBM864, true, csIBM864, ibm-864, ibm864, 864, cp864
IBM865, IBM865, true, ibm-865, csIBM865, cp865, ibm865, 865
IBM866, IBM866, true, ibm866, 866, ibm-866, csIBM866, cp866
IBM868, IBM868, true, ibm868, 868, cp868, csIBM868, ibm-868, cp-ar
IBM869, IBM869, true, cp869, ibm869, 869, ibm-869, cp-gr, csIBM869
IBM870, IBM870, true, 870, cp870, csIBM870, ibm-870, ibm870, ebcdic-cp-...
IBM871, IBM871, true, ibm871, 871, cp871, ebcdic-cp-is, csIBM871, ibm-871
IBM918, IBM918, true, 918, ibm-918, ebcdic-cp-ar2, cp918
ISO-2022-CN, ISO-2022-CN, false, csISO2022CN, ISO2022CN
ISO-2022-JP, ISO-2022-JP, true, csjisencoding, iso2022jp, jis_encoding, ...
ISO-2022-JP-2, ISO-2022-JP-2, true, csISO2022JP2, iso2022jp2
ISO-2022-KR, ISO-2022-KR, true, csISO2022KR, ISO2022KR
ISO-8859-1, ISO-8859-1, true, 819, ISO8859-1, l1, ISO_8859-1:1987, ...
ISO-8859-13, ISO-8859-13, true, iso_8859-13, ISO8859-13, iso8859_13, ...
ISO-8859-15, ISO-8859-15, true, csISO885915, Latin-9, ISO8859-15, ...
ISO-8859-16, ISO-8859-16, true, ISO_8859-16:2001, latin10, iso-ir-226,...
ISO-8859-2, ISO-8859-2, true, ISO8859-2, ibm912, l2, ISO_8859-2, 8859_...
ISO-8859-3, ISO-8859-3, true, ISO8859-3, ibm913, 8859_3, l3, cp913, ...
ISO-8859-4, ISO-8859-4, true, 8859_4, latin4, l4, cp914, ISO_8859-4...
ISO-8859-5, ISO-8859-5, true, ISO_8859-5:1988, csISOLatinCyrillic, ...
ISO-8859-6, ISO-8859-6, true, ASMO-708, 8859_6, iso8859_6, ISO_8859-6,...
ISO-8859-7, ISO-8859-7, true, greek, 8859_7, greek8, ibm813, ISO_8859-...
ISO-8859-8, ISO-8859-8, true, 8859_8, ISO_8859-8, ISO_8859-8:1988, ...
ISO-8859-9, ISO-8859-9, true, ibm-920, ISO_8859-9, 8859_9, ISO_8859-:...
JIS_X0201, JIS_X0201, true, JIS0201, csHalfWidthKatakana, X0201, JIS_...
JIS_X0212-1990, JIS_X0212-1990, true, JIS0212, iso-ir-159, x0212, jis_...
KOI8-R, KOI8-R, true, koi8_r, koi8, cskoi8r
KOI8-U, KOI8-U, true, koi8_u
Shift_JIS, Shift_JIS, true, shift_jis, x-sjis, sjis, shift-jis, ...
TIS-620, TIS-620, true, tis620, tis620.2533
US-ASCII, US-ASCII, true, ANSI_X3.4-1968, cp367, csASCII, iso-ir-6, ...
UTF-16, UTF-16, true, UTF_16, unicode, utf16, UnicodeBig
UTF-16BE, UTF-16BE, true, X-UTF-16BE, UTF_16BE, ISO-10646-UCS-2, ...
UTF-16LE, UTF-16LE, true, UnicodeLittleUnmarked, UTF_16LE, X-UTF-16LE
UTF-32, UTF-32, true, UTF_32, UTF32
UTF-32BE, UTF-32BE, true, X-UTF-32BE, UTF_32BE
```

```
UTF-32LE, UTF-32LE, true, X-UTF-32LE, UTF_32LE

UTF-8, UTF-8, true, unicode-1-1-utf-8, UTF8

windows-1250, windows-1250, true, cp1250, cp5346

windows-1251, windows-1251, true, cp5347, ansi-1251, cp1251

windows-1252, windows-1252, true, ibm-1252, cp1252, ibm1252, cp5348

windows-1253, windows-1253, true, cp1253, cp5349

windows-1254, windows-1254, true, cp1254, cp5350

windows-1255, windows-1255, true, cp1255

windows-1256, windows-1256, true, cp1256

windows-1257, windows-1257, true, cp1257, cp5353

windows-1258, windows-1258, true, cp1258

windows-31j, windows-31j, true, MS932, windows-932, csWindows31J

x-Big5-HKSCS-2001, x-Big5-HKSCS-2001, true, Big5_HKSCS_2001, big5-...

x-Big5-Solaris, x-Big5-Solaris, true, Big5_Solaris

x-euc-jp-linux, x-euc-jp-linux, true, euc_jp_linux, euc-jp-linux

x-EUC-TW, x-EUC-TW, true, euctw, cns11643, EUC-TW, euc_tw

x-eucJP-Open, x-eucJP-Open, true, eucJP-open, EUC_JP_Solaris


x-IBM1006, x-IBM1006, true, ibm1006, ibm-1006, 1006, cp1006

x-IBM1025, x-IBM1025, true, ibm-1025, 1025, cp1025, ibm1025

x-IBM1046, x-IBM1046, true, ibm1046, ibm-1046, 1046, cp1046

x-IBM1097, x-IBM1097, true, ibm1097, ibm-1097, 1097, cp1097

x-IBM1098, x-IBM1098, true, ibm-1098, 1098, cp1098, ibm1098

x-IBM1112, x-IBM1112, true, ibm1112, ibm-1112, 1112, cp1112

x-IBM1122, x-IBM1122, true, cp1122, ibm1122, ibm-1122, 1122

x-IBM1123, x-IBM1123, true, ibm1123, ibm-1123, 1123, cp1123

x-IBM1124, x-IBM1124, true, ibm-1124, 1124, cp1124, ibm1124

x-IBM1166, x-IBM1166, true, cp1166, ibm1166, ibm-1166, 1166

x-IBM1364, x-IBM1364, true, cp1364, ibm1364, ibm-1364, 1364

x-IBM1381, x-IBM1381, true, cp1381, ibm-1381, 1381, ibm1381

x-IBM1383, x-IBM1383, true, ibm1383, ibm-1383, 1383, cp1383, cpeuccn, ...

x-IBM300, x-IBM300, true, cp300, ibm300, 300, ibm-300

x-IBM33722, x-IBM33722, true, 33722, ibm-33722, cp33722, ibm33722, ...

x-IBM737, x-IBM737, true, cp737, ibm737, 737, ibm-737

x-IBM833, x-IBM833, true, ibm833, cp833, ibm-833

x-IBM834, x-IBM834, true, ibm834, 834, cp834, ibm-834

x-IBM856, x-IBM856, true, ibm856, 856, cp856, ibm-856

x-IBM874, x-IBM874, true, ibm-874, ibm874, 874, cp874
```

```
x-IBM875, x-IBM875, true, ibm-875, ibm875, 875, cp875
x-IBM921, x-IBM921, true, ibm921, 921, ibm-921, cp921
x-IBM922, x-IBM922, true, ibm922, 922, cp922, ibm-922
x-IBM930, x-IBM930, true, ibm-930, ibm930, 930, cp930
x-IBM933, x-IBM933, true, ibm933, 933, cp933, ibm-933
x-IBM935, x-IBM935, true, cp935, ibm935, 935, ibm-935
x-IBM937, x-IBM937, true, ibm-937, ibm937, 937, cp937
x-IBM939, x-IBM939, true, ibm-939, cp939, ibm939, 939
x-IBM942, x-IBM942, true, ibm-942, cp942, ibm942, 942
x-IBM942C, x-IBM942C, true, ibm932, x-ibm932, ibm-932, ibm942C, ...
x-IBM943, x-IBM943, true, ibm943, 943, ibm-943, cp943
x-IBM943C, x-IBM943C, true, 943C, cp943C, ibm943C, ibm-943C
x-IBM948, x-IBM948, true, ibm-948, ibm948, 948, cp948
x-IBM949, x-IBM949, true, ibm-949, ibm949, 949, cp949
x-IBM949C, x-IBM949C, true, ibm949C, ibm-949C, cp949C, 949C
x-IBM950, x-IBM950, true, cp950, ibm950, 950, ibm-950
x-IBM964, x-IBM964, true, ibm-964, cp964, ibm964, 964
x-IBM970, x-IBM970, true, ibm970, ibm-eucKR, 970, cp970, ibm-970
x-ISCII91, x-ISCII91, true, ISCII91, iso-ir-153, iscii, ...
x-ISO-2022-CN-CNS, x-ISO-2022-CN-CNS, true, ISO2022CN_CNS, ...
x-ISO-2022-CN-GB, x-ISO-2022-CN-GB, true, ISO2022CN_GB, ...
x-iso-8859-11, x-iso-8859-11, true, iso-8859-11, iso8859_11
x-JIS0208, x-JIS0208, true, JIS0208, JIS_C6226-1983, iso-ir-87, ...
x-JISAutoDetect, x-JISAutoDetect, false, JISAutoDetect
x-Johab, x-Johab, true, ms1361, ksc5601_1992, johab, ksc5601-1992
x-MacArabic, x-MacArabic, true, MacArabic
x-MacCentralEurope, x-MacCentralEurope, true, MacCentralEurope
x-MacCroatian, x-MacCroatian, true, MacCroatian
x-MacCyrillic, x-MacCyrillic, true, MacCyrillic
x-MacDingbat, x-MacDingbat, true, MacDingbat
x-MacGreek, x-MacGreek, true, MacGreek
x-MacHebrew, x-MacHebrew, true, MacHebrew
x-MacIceland, x-MacIceland, true, MacIceland
x-MacRoman, x-MacRoman, true, MacRoman
x-MacRomania, x-MacRomania, true, MacRomania
x-MacSymbol, x-MacSymbol, true, MacSymbol
x-MacThai, x-MacThai, true, MacThai
```

```
x-MacTurkish, x-MacTurkish, true, MacTurkish
x-MacUkraine, x-MacUkraine, true, MacUkraine
x-MS932_0213, x-MS932_0213, true, MS932:2004, windows-932:2004, ...
x-MS950-HKSCS, x-MS950-HKSCS, true, MS950_HKSCS
x-MS950-HKSCS-XP, x-MS950-HKSCS-XP, true, MS950_HKSCS_XP
x-mswin-936, x-mswin-936, true, ms936, ms_936
x-PCK, x-PCK, true, pck
x-SJIS_0213, x-SJIS_0213, true, shift_jis:2004, sjis_0213, ...
x-UTF-16LE-BOM, x-UTF-16LE-BOM, true, UnicodeLittle
X-UTF-32BE-BOM, X-UTF-32BE-BOM, true, UTF_32BE_BOM, UTF-32BE-BOM
X-UTF-32LE-BOM, X-UTF-32LE-BOM, true, UTF_32LE_BOM, UTF-32LE-BOM
x-windows-50220, x-windows-50220, true, cp50220, ms50220
x-windows-50221, x-windows-50221, true, cp50221, ms50221
x-windows-874, x-windows-874, true, ms-874, ms874, windows-874
x-windows-949, x-windows-949, true, windows949, ms949, windows-949, ...
x-windows-950, x-windows-950, true, ms950, windows-950
x-windows-iso2022jp, x-windows-iso2022jp, true, windows-iso2022jp
```

The output is very impressive. Java supports a total of 172 character encodings!

EncodingSampler.java - Testing encode() Methods

This section provides a tutorial example on how to use 4 different methods provided in Java to encode characters with a given character encoding.

Java offers 4 methods to perform character encoding:

- CharsetEncoder.encode()

- Charset.encode()

- String.getBytes()

- OutputStreamWriter.write()

Here is a program that demonstrate how to encode characters with each of above 4 methods:

```
/* EncodingSampler2.java
```

```
 * Copyright (c) 2019 HerongYang.com. All Rights Reserved.
 */
import java.io.*;
import java.nio.*;
import java.nio.charset.*;
class EncodingSampler2 {
   static String dfltCharset = null;
   static int[] chars={0x0000, 0x003F, 0x0040, 0x007F, 0x0080, 0x00BF,
                       0x00C0, 0x00FF, 0x0100, 0x3FFF, 0x4000, 0x7FFF,
                       0x8000, 0xBFFF, 0xC000, 0xEFFF, 0xF000, 0xFFFF,
                       0x1F108, 0x1F132, 0x1F1A0};
   static char hexDigit[] = {'0', '1', '2', '3', '4', '5', '6', '7',
                             '8', '9', 'A', 'B', 'C', 'D', 'E', 'F'};
   public static void main(String[] arg) {
      String charset = null;
      if (arg.length>0) charset = arg[0];
      OutputStreamWriter o = new OutputStreamWriter(
         new ByteArrayOutputStream());
      dfltCharset = o.getEncoding();
      if (charset==null) System.out.println("Default ("+dfltCharset
         +") encoding:");
      else System.out.println(charset+" encoding:");
      System.out.println("Char,    String, Writer, Charset, Encoder");
      for (int i=0; i<chars.length; i++) {
         int c = chars[i];
         byte[] b1 = encodeByString(c,charset);
         byte[] b2 = encodeByWriter(c,charset);
         byte[] b3 = encodeByCharset(c,charset);
         byte[] b4 = encodeByEncoder(c,charset);
         System.out.print(intToHex(c)+",");
         printBytes(b1);
         System.out.print(",");
         printBytes(b2);
         System.out.print(",");
         printBytes(b3);
         System.out.print(",");
         printBytes(b4);
```

```
            System.out.println("");
        }
    }
    public static byte[] encodeByCharset(int c, String cs) {
        Charset cso = null;
        byte[] b = null;
        try {
            if (cs==null) cso = Charset.forName(dfltCharset);
            else cso = Charset.forName(cs);
            ByteBuffer bb = cso.encode(new String(Character.toChars(c)));
            b = copyBytes(bb.array(),bb.limit());
        } catch (IllegalCharsetNameException e) {
            System.out.println(e.toString());
        }
        return b;
    }
    public static byte[] encodeByEncoder(int c, String cs) {
        Charset cso = null;
        byte[] b = null;
        try {
            if (cs==null) cso = Charset.forName(dfltCharset);
            else cso = Charset.forName(cs);
            CharsetEncoder e =  cso.newEncoder();
            e.reset();
            ByteBuffer bb
               = e.encode(CharBuffer.wrap(Character.toChars(c)));
            b = copyBytes(bb.array(),bb.limit());
        } catch (IllegalCharsetNameException e) {
            System.out.println(e.toString());
        } catch (CharacterCodingException e) {
            //System.out.println(e.toString());
            b = new byte[] {(byte)0x00};
        }
        return b;
    }
    public static byte[] encodeByString(int c, String cs) {
        String s = new String(Character.toChars(c));
```

```
    byte[] b = null;
    if (cs==null) {
        b = s.getBytes();
    } else {
        try {
            b = s.getBytes(cs);
        } catch (UnsupportedEncodingException e) {
            System.out.println(e.toString());
        }
    }
    return b;
}
public static byte[] encodeByWriter(int c, String cs) {
    byte[] b = null;
    ByteArrayOutputStream bs = new ByteArrayOutputStream();
    OutputStreamWriter o = null;
    if (cs==null) {
        o = new OutputStreamWriter(bs);
    } else {
        try {
            o = new OutputStreamWriter(bs, cs);
        } catch (UnsupportedEncodingException e) {
            System.out.println(e.toString());
        }
    }
    String s = new String(Character.toChars(c));
    try {
        o.write(s);
        o.flush();
        b = bs.toByteArray();
        o.close();
    } catch (IOException e) {
        System.out.println(e.toString());
    }
    return b;
}
public static byte[] copyBytes(byte[] a, int l) {
```

```
        byte[] b = new byte[l];
        for (int i=0; i<Math.min(l,a.length); i++) b[i] = a[i];
        return b;
    }
    public static void printBytes(byte[] b) {
        for (int j=0; j<b.length; j++)
            System.out.print(" "+byteToHex(b[j]));
    }
    public static String byteToHex(byte b) {
        char[] a = { hexDigit[(b >> 4) & 0x0f], hexDigit[b & 0x0f] };
        return new String(a);
    }
    public static String charToHex(char c) {
        byte hi = (byte) (c >>> 8);
        byte lo = (byte) (c & 0xff);
        return byteToHex(hi) + byteToHex(lo);
    }
    public static String intToHex(int i) {
        char hi = (char) (i >>> 16);
        char lo = (char) (i & 0xffff);
        return charToHex(hi) + charToHex(lo);
    }
}
```

Note that:

- If the same encoding is used, all 4 methods: encodeByString(), encodeByWriter(), encodeByCharset() and encodeByEncoder(), should return the exactly the same byte sequence.

- getEncoding() is used on OutputStreamWriter class to get the name of the default encoding.

- There is no way to know the name of the default encoding on String class.

- There is no default instance of Charset and Encoder.

- If the given character is not part of the character set of the encoding, the CharsetEncoder.encode() method will return 0x00, the NULL character.

- If the given character is not part of the character set of the encoding, Charset.encode(), String.getBytes(), and OutputStreamWriter.write() methods will all return 0x3F, the "?" character.

Examples of CP1252 and ISO-8859-1 Encodings

This section provides examples of encoded byte sequences of the JVM default encoding, CP1252 encoding, on a Windows system. The ISO-8859-1 encoding is slightly different that the CP1252 encoding.

Running the testing program with Java 11, EncodingSampler2.java, provided in the previous section without any argument will use the JVM's default character encoding:

```
C:\herong>javac EncodingSampler2.java

C:\herong>java EncodingSampler2
Default (Cp1252) encoding:
Char,     String, Writer, Charset, Encoder
00000000, 00, 00, 00, 00
0000003F, 3F, 3F, 3F, 3F
00000040, 40, 40, 40, 40
0000007F, 7F, 7F, 7F, 7F
00000080, 3F, 3F, 3F, 00
000000BF, BF, BF, BF, BF
000000C0, C0, C0, C0, C0
000000FF, FF, FF, FF, FF
00000100, 3F, 3F, 3F, 00
00003FFF, 3F, 3F, 3F, 00
00004000, 3F, 3F, 3F, 00
00007FFF, 3F, 3F, 3F, 00
00008000, 3F, 3F, 3F, 00
0000BFFF, 3F, 3F, 3F, 00
0000C000, 3F, 3F, 3F, 00
0000EFFF, 3F, 3F, 3F, 00
0000F000, 3F, 3F, 3F, 00
0000FFFF, 3F, 3F, 3F, 00
```

```
0001F108, 3F, 3F, 3F, 00
0001F132, 3F, 3F, 3F, 00
0001F1A0, 3F, 3F, 3F, 00
```

The results shows that:

- The default encoding of the String class seems to be the same as OutputStreamWriter: Cp1252.

- It seems that characters with code points higher than 0x00FF are not part of the Cp1252 character set. This why we are getting 0x3F, the "?" character, from Charset.encode(), String.getBytes(), and OutputStreamWriter.write() methods on 0x0100 and other high code points characters.

- Some characters in the 0x0000 - 0x00FF range are also not part of the Cp1252 character set. For example, 0x80.

Running the program again with 'CP1252' as the argument should give us the same output as the previous run:

```
C:\herong>java EncodingSampler2 CP1252
CP1252 encoding:
Char,     String, Writer, Charset, Encoder
00000000, 00, 00, 00, 00
0000003F, 3F, 3F, 3F, 3F
00000040, 40, 40, 40, 40
0000007F, 7F, 7F, 7F, 7F
00000080, 3F, 3F, 3F, 00
000000BF, BF, BF, BF, BF
000000C0, C0, C0, C0, C0
000000FF, FF, FF, FF, FF
00000100, 3F, 3F, 3F, 00
00003FFF, 3F, 3F, 3F, 00
00004000, 3F, 3F, 3F, 00
00007FFF, 3F, 3F, 3F, 00
00008000, 3F, 3F, 3F, 00
0000BFFF, 3F, 3F, 3F, 00
0000C000, 3F, 3F, 3F, 00
0000EFFF, 3F, 3F, 3F, 00
0000F000, 3F, 3F, 3F, 00
```

```
0000FFFF, 3F, 3F, 3F, 00
0001F108, 3F, 3F, 3F, 00
0001F132, 3F, 3F, 3F, 00
0001F1A0, 3F, 3F, 3F, 00
```

Let's try another encoding, ISO-8859-1:

```
C:\herong>java EncodingSampler2 ISO-8859-1
ISO-8859-1 encoding:
Char, String, Writer, Charset, Encoder
ISO-8859-1 encoding:
Char,      String, Writer, Charset, Encoder
00000000, 00, 00, 00, 00
0000003F, 3F, 3F, 3F, 3F
00000040, 40, 40, 40, 40
0000007F, 7F, 7F, 7F, 7F
00000080, 80, 80, 80, 80
000000BF, BF, BF, BF, BF
000000C0, C0, C0, C0, C0
000000FF, FF, FF, FF, FF
00000100, 3F, 3F, 3F, 00
00003FFF, 3F, 3F, 3F, 00
00004000, 3F, 3F, 3F, 00
00007FFF, 3F, 3F, 3F, 00
00008000, 3F, 3F, 3F, 00
0000BFFF, 3F, 3F, 3F, 00
0000C000, 3F, 3F, 3F, 00
0000EFFF, 3F, 3F, 3F, 00
0000F000, 3F, 3F, 3F, 00
0000FFFF, 3F, 3F, 3F, 00
0001F108, 3F, 3F, 3F, 00
0001F132, 3F, 3F, 3F, 00
0001F1A0, 3F, 3F, 3F, 00
```

ISO-8859-1 encoding is different than CP1252 encoding. As you can see in the output, 0x80 is a valid character in the ISO-8859-1 character set, but not valid in the CP1252 character set.

Examples of US-ASCII, UTF-8, UTF-16 and UTF-32 Encodings

This section provides examples of encoded byte sequences of US-ASCII, UTF-8, UTF-16, UTF-16BE, UTF-32BE encodings.

Let's continue to play with the testing program, EncodingSampler2.java, provided in the previous section. This time, I want to try the US-ASCII encoding:

```
C:\herong>java EncodingSampler2 US-ASCII
US-ASCII encoding:
Char,     String, Writer, Charset, Encoder
00000000, 00, 00, 00, 00
0000003F, 3F, 3F, 3F, 3F
00000040, 40, 40, 40, 40
0000007F, 7F, 7F, 7F, 7F
00000080, 3F, 3F, 3F, 00
000000BF, 3F, 3F, 3F, 00
000000C0, 3F, 3F, 3F, 00
000000FF, 3F, 3F, 3F, 00
00000100, 3F, 3F, 3F, 00
00003FFF, 3F, 3F, 3F, 00
00004000, 3F, 3F, 3F, 00
00007FFF, 3F, 3F, 3F, 00
00008000, 3F, 3F, 3F, 00
0000BFFF, 3F, 3F, 3F, 00
0000C000, 3F, 3F, 3F, 00
0000EFFF, 3F, 3F, 3F, 00
0000F000, 3F, 3F, 3F, 00
0000FFFF, 3F, 3F, 3F, 00
0001F108, 3F, 3F, 3F, 00
0001F132, 3F, 3F, 3F, 00
0001F1A0, 3F, 3F, 3F, 00
```

It's obvious that US-ASCII works on a character set in the 0x0000 - 0x007F range.

Now I wan to try the UTF-8 encoding, which should be compatible with the US-ASCII encoding:

```
C:\herong>java EncodingSampler2 UTF-8
UTF-8 encoding:
Char,      String, Writer, Charset, Encoder
00000000, 00, 00, 00, 00
0000003F, 3F, 3F, 3F, 3F
00000040, 40, 40, 40, 40
0000007F, 7F, 7F, 7F, 7F
00000080, C2 80, C2 80, C2 80, C2 80
000000BF, C2 BF, C2 BF, C2 BF, C2 BF
000000C0, C3 80, C3 80, C3 80, C3 80
000000FF, C3 BF, C3 BF, C3 BF, C3 BF
00000100, C4 80, C4 80, C4 80, C4 80
00003FFF, E3 BF BF, E3 BF BF, E3 BF BF, E3 BF BF
00004000, E4 80 80, E4 80 80, E4 80 80, E4 80 80
00007FFF, E7 BF BF, E7 BF BF, E7 BF BF, E7 BF BF
00008000, E8 80 80, E8 80 80, E8 80 80, E8 80 80
0000BFFF, EB BF BF, EB BF BF, EB BF BF, EB BF BF
0000C000, EC 80 80, EC 80 80, EC 80 80, EC 80 80
0000EFFF, EE BF BF, EE BF BF, EE BF BF, EE BF BF
0000F000, EF 80 80, EF 80 80, EF 80 80, EF 80 80
0000FFFF, EF BF BF, EF BF BF, EF BF BF, EF BF BF
0001F108, F0 9F 84 88, F0 9F 84 88, F0 9F 84 88, F0 9F 84 88
0001F132, F0 9F 84 B2, F0 9F 84 B2, F0 9F 84 B2, F0 9F 84 B2
0001F1A0, F0 9F 86 A0, F0 9F 86 A0, F0 9F 86 A0, F0 9F 86 A0
```

The output matches my expectation.

Let's try another Unicode encoding, UTF-16:

```
C:\herong>java EncodingSampler2 UTF-16
UTF-16 encoding:
Char,      String, Writer, Charset, Encoder
00000000, FE FF 00 00, FE FF 00 00, FE FF 00 00, FE FF 00 00
0000003F, FE FF 00 3F, FE FF 00 3F, FE FF 00 3F, FE FF 00 3F
00000040, FE FF 00 40, FE FF 00 40, FE FF 00 40, FE FF 00 40
0000007F, FE FF 00 7F, FE FF 00 7F, FE FF 00 7F, FE FF 00 7F
```

```
00000080, FE FF 00 80, FE FF 00 80, FE FF 00 80, FE FF 00 80
000000BF, FE FF 00 BF, FE FF 00 BF, FE FF 00 BF, FE FF 00 BF
000000C0, FE FF 00 C0, FE FF 00 C0, FE FF 00 C0, FE FF 00 C0
000000FF, FE FF 00 FF, FE FF 00 FF, FE FF 00 FF, FE FF 00 FF
00000100, FE FF 01 00, FE FF 01 00, FE FF 01 00, FE FF 01 00
00003FFF, FE FF 3F FF, FE FF 3F FF, FE FF 3F FF, FE FF 3F FF
00004000, FE FF 40 00, FE FF 40 00, FE FF 40 00, FE FF 40 00
00007FFF, FE FF 7F FF, FE FF 7F FF, FE FF 7F FF, FE FF 7F FF
00008000, FE FF 80 00, FE FF 80 00, FE FF 80 00, FE FF 80 00
0000BFFF, FE FF BF FF, FE FF BF FF, FE FF BF FF, FE FF BF FF
0000C000, FE FF C0 00, FE FF C0 00, FE FF C0 00, FE FF C0 00
0000EFFF, FE FF EF FF, FE FF EF FF, FE FF EF FF, FE FF EF FF
0000F000, FE FF F0 00, FE FF F0 00, FE FF F0 00, FE FF F0 00
0000FFFF, FE FF FF FF, FE FF FF FF, FE FF FF FF, FE FF FF FF
0001F108, FE FF D8 3C DD 08, FE FF D8 3C DD 08, FE FF D8 3C DD 08, ...
0001F132, FE FF D8 3C DD 32, FE FF D8 3C DD 32, FE FF D8 3C DD 32, ...
0001F1A0, FE FF D8 3C DD A0, FE FF D8 3C DD A0, FE FF D8 3C DD A0, ...
```

Noticed that the first 2 bytes, 0xFEFF, of the encoding output is a BOM (Byte Order Mark) indicates that the following byte sequence is in Big Endian format. In other words, Java uses the "Big-Endian with BOM" format for UTF-16 encoding by default.

How about UTF-16BE encoding:

```
C:\herong>java EncodingSampler2 UTF-16BE
UTF-16BE encoding:
Char,      String, Writer, Charset, Encoder
00000000, 00 00, 00 00, 00 00, 00 00
0000003F, 00 3F, 00 3F, 00 3F, 00 3F
00000040, 00 40, 00 40, 00 40, 00 40
0000007F, 00 7F, 00 7F, 00 7F, 00 7F
00000080, 00 80, 00 80, 00 80, 00 80
000000BF, 00 BF, 00 BF, 00 BF, 00 BF
000000C0, 00 C0, 00 C0, 00 C0, 00 C0
000000FF, 00 FF, 00 FF, 00 FF, 00 FF
00000100, 01 00, 01 00, 01 00, 01 00
00003FFF, 3F FF, 3F FF, 3F FF, 3F FF
00004000, 40 00, 40 00, 40 00, 40 00
00007FFF, 7F FF, 7F FF, 7F FF, 7F FF
```

```
00008000, 80 00, 80 00, 80 00, 80 00
0000BFFF, BF FF, BF FF, BF FF, BF FF
0000C000, C0 00, C0 00, C0 00, C0 00
0000EFFF, EF FF, EF FF, EF FF, EF FF
0000F000, F0 00, F0 00, F0 00, F0 00
0000FFFF, FF FF, FF FF, FF FF, FF FF
0001F108, D8 3C DD 08, D8 3C DD 08, D8 3C DD 08, D8 3C DD 08
0001F132, D8 3C DD 32, D8 3C DD 32, D8 3C DD 32, D8 3C DD 32
0001F1A0, D8 3C DD A0, D8 3C DD A0, D8 3C DD A0, D8 3C DD A0
```

Notice that how characters in the 0x10000 - 0x10FFFF range are encoded into 32 bits, or 16-bit pairs.

The last Unicode encoding to look at is the UTF-32BE encoding:

```
C:\herong>java EncodingSampler2 UTF-32BE
UTF-32BE encoding:
Char,      String, Writer, Charset, Encoder
00000000, 00 00 00 00, 00 00 00 00, 00 00 00 00, 00 00 00 00
0000003F, 00 00 00 3F, 00 00 00 3F, 00 00 00 3F, 00 00 00 3F
00000040, 00 00 00 40, 00 00 00 40, 00 00 00 40, 00 00 00 40
0000007F, 00 00 00 7F, 00 00 00 7F, 00 00 00 7F, 00 00 00 7F
00000080, 00 00 00 80, 00 00 00 80, 00 00 00 80, 00 00 00 80
000000BF, 00 00 00 BF, 00 00 00 BF, 00 00 00 BF, 00 00 00 BF
000000C0, 00 00 00 C0, 00 00 00 C0, 00 00 00 C0, 00 00 00 C0
000000FF, 00 00 00 FF, 00 00 00 FF, 00 00 00 FF, 00 00 00 FF
00000100, 00 00 01 00, 00 00 01 00, 00 00 01 00, 00 00 01 00
00003FFF, 00 00 3F FF, 00 00 3F FF, 00 00 3F FF, 00 00 3F FF
00004000, 00 00 40 00, 00 00 40 00, 00 00 40 00, 00 00 40 00
00007FFF, 00 00 7F FF, 00 00 7F FF, 00 00 7F FF, 00 00 7F FF
00008000, 00 00 80 00, 00 00 80 00, 00 00 80 00, 00 00 80 00
0000BFFF, 00 00 BF FF, 00 00 BF FF, 00 00 BF FF, 00 00 BF FF
0000C000, 00 00 C0 00, 00 00 C0 00, 00 00 C0 00, 00 00 C0 00
0000EFFF, 00 00 EF FF, 00 00 EF FF, 00 00 EF FF, 00 00 EF FF
0000F000, 00 00 F0 00, 00 00 F0 00, 00 00 F0 00, 00 00 F0 00
0000FFFF, 00 00 FF FF, 00 00 FF FF, 00 00 FF FF, 00 00 FF FF
0001F108, 00 01 F1 08, 00 01 F1 08, 00 01 F1 08, 00 01 F1 08
0001F132, 00 01 F1 32, 00 01 F1 32, 00 01 F1 32, 00 01 F1 32
```

```
0001F1A0, 00 01 F1 A0, 00 01 F1 A0, 00 01 F1 A0, 00 01 F1 A0
```

Obviously, UTF-32BE encoding is much simpler and very easy to understand than UTF-16BE and UTF-8 encodings.

Examples of GB18030 Encoding

This section provides examples of encoded byte sequences of GB18030 encoding, which is designed to encode Chinese characters.

Let's continue to play with the testing program, EncodingSampler2.java, provided in the previous section with GB18030 encoding for Chinese characters:

```
C:\herong>java EncodingSampler2 GB18030
GB18030 encoding:
Char,      String, Writer, Charset, Encoder
00000000, 00, 00, 00, 00
0000003F, 3F, 3F, 3F, 3F
00000040, 40, 40, 40, 40
0000007F, 7F, 7F, 7F, 7F
00000080, 81 30 81 30, 81 30 81 30, 81 30 81 30, 81 30 81 30
000000BF, 81 30 86 37, 81 30 86 37, 81 30 86 37, 81 30 86 37
000000C0, 81 30 86 38, 81 30 86 38, 81 30 86 38, 81 30 86 38
000000FF, 81 30 8B 37, 81 30 8B 37, 81 30 8B 37, 81 30 8B 37
00000100, 81 30 8B 38, 81 30 8B 38, 81 30 8B 38, 81 30 8B 38
00003FFF, 82 32 A6 36, 82 32 A6 36, 82 32 A6 36, 82 32 A6 36
00004000, 82 32 A6 37, 82 32 A6 37, 82 32 A6 37, 82 32 A6 37
00007FFF, C2 52, C2 52, C2 52, C2 52
00008000, D2 AB, D2 AB, D2 AB, D2 AB
0000BFFF, 83 31 D7 34, 83 31 D7 34, 83 31 D7 34, 83 31 D7 34
0000C000, 83 31 D7 35, 83 31 D7 35, 83 31 D7 35, 83 31 D7 35
0000EFFF, 83 38 96 36, 83 38 96 36, 83 38 96 36, 83 38 96 36
0000F000, 83 38 96 37, 83 38 96 37, 83 38 96 37, 83 38 96 37
0000FFFF, 84 31 A4 39, 84 31 A4 39, 84 31 A4 39, 84 31 A4 39
0001F108, 94 38 FB 34, 94 38 FB 34, 94 38 FB 34, 94 38 FB 34
0001F132, 94 39 81 36, 94 39 81 36, 94 39 81 36, 94 39 81 36
```

```
0001F1A0, 94 39 8C 36, 94 39 8C 36, 94 39 8C 36, 94 39 8C 36
```

It looks complicated.

I think that's enough. You can run the test program with any other supported encodings as an argument yourself.

Testing decode() Methods

This section describes 4 different methods provided in Java to decode byte sequences back to characters with a given encoding.

There are 4 methods provided in Java 11 to decode characters:

- CharsetDecoder.decode()

- Charset.decode()

- new String()

- InputStreamReader.read()

The way to use those methods is similar to encode methods described in previous sections.

Exercise: Write a Java program to decode byte sequences back to Unicode character code points.

Character Set Encoding Maps

This chapter provides tutorial notes and example codes on character set encoding maps. Topics include collection types: encoding map analyzer program; analyzing and print encoding maps for US-ASCII, ISO-8859-1/Latin 1, Windows CP1252, Unicode UTF-8, UTF-16, UTF-32; sample program to count valid characters in each character set encoding.

Conclusion:

- A simple Java program can be used to print the encoding map of any given encoding supported by Java.

- US-ASCII encoding has a code point range of 0x0000 - 0x007F.

- ISO-8859-1/Latin 1 encoding has a code point range of 0x0000 - 0x00FF.

- CP1252/Windows-1252 encoding has a code point range of 0x0000 - 0x00FF plus some values outside this range.

- UTF-8, UTF-16, and UTF-32 encodings are Unicode standard encodings with valid code points in the range of 0x0000 - 0x10FFFF.

- A simple Java program can be used to count valid characters of any given encoding.

Character Set Encoding Map Analyzer

This section provides a tutorial example on how to write a simple program to analyze and print out the encoding map showing relations between character code points and their encoded byte sequences of a given encoding.

As mentioned in the previous chapter, Java 11 supports 171 built-in character set encodings.

In order to figure out the encoding map (relations between character code points and their encoded byte sequences) of a specific supported encoding, I wrote the following program to analyze a given encoding and print a map between code points (from 0x0000 to 0x10FFFF) and their encoded byte sequences:

```java
/* EncodingAnalyzer2.java
 * Copyright (c) 2019 HerongYang.com. All Rights Reserved.
 */
import java.io.*;
class EncodingAnalyzer2 {
    static char hexDigit[] = {'0', '1', '2', '3', '4', '5', '6', '7',
                              '8', '9', 'A', 'B', 'C', 'D', 'E', 'F'};
    public static void main(String[] a) {
        String charset = null;
        if (a.length>0) charset = a[0];
        if (charset==null) System.out.println("Default encoding:");
        else System.out.println(charset+" encoding:");
        int lastByte = 0;
        int lastLength = 0;
        byte[] startSequence = null;
        int startChar = 0;
        byte[] endSequence = null;
        int endChar = 0;
        boolean isFirstChar = true;
        for (int i=0; i<=0x10FFFF; i++) {
            int c = i;
            String s = new String(Character.toChars(c));
            byte[] b = null;
```

```
      if (charset==null) {
         b = s.getBytes();
      } else {
         try {
            b = s.getBytes(charset);
         } catch (UnsupportedEncodingException e) {
            System.out.println(e.toString());
            break;
         }
      }
      int l = b.length;
      int lb = ((int) b[l-1]) & 0x00FF;
      if (isFirstChar==true) {
         isFirstChar = false;
         startSequence = b;
         startChar = c;
         lastByte = lb - 1;
         lastLength = l;
      }
      if (!(l==lastLength && (lb==lastByte+1 || lb==lastByte))) {
         System.out.print(intToHex(startChar)+" >");
         printBytes(startSequence);
         System.out.print(" - "+intToHex(endChar)+" >");
         printBytes(endSequence);
         if (lastByte==0x3F) System.out.print(": Invalid range");
         System.out.println("");
         startSequence = b;
         startChar = c;
      }
      endSequence = b;
      endChar = c;
      lastLength = l;
      lastByte = lb;
   }
   System.out.print(intToHex(startChar)+" >");
   printBytes(startSequence);
   System.out.print(" - "+intToHex(endChar)+" >");
```

```
        printBytes(endSequence);
        if (lastByte==0x3F) System.out.print(": Invalid range");
        System.out.println("");
    }
    public static void printBytes(byte[] b) {
        for (int j=0; j<b.length; j++)
            System.out.print(" "+byteToHex(b[j]));
    }
    public static String byteToHex(byte b) {
        char[] a = { hexDigit[(b >> 4) & 0x0f], hexDigit[b & 0x0f] };
        return new String(a);
    }
    public static String charToHex(char c) {
        byte hi = (byte) (c >>> 8);
        byte lo = (byte) (c & 0xff);
        return byteToHex(hi) + byteToHex(lo);
    }
    public static String intToHex(int i) {
        char hi = (char) (i >>> 16);
        char lo = (char) (i & 0xffff);
        return charToHex(hi) + charToHex(lo);
    }
}
```

Note that:

- String.getBytes() is used to encode the code point stored in the String object.

- The encoding name should be specified as command argument.

The output of this program will be discussed in sections bellow.

Character Set Encoding Maps - US-ASCII and ISO-8859-1/Latin 1

This section provides a tutorial example of analyzing and printing character set encoding maps for 2 encodings: US-ASCII and ISO-8859-1/Latin 1.

Here is the output of my sample program, EncodingAnalyzer2.java, for US-ASCII encoding with Java SE 7:

```
C:\herong>javac EncodingAnalyzer2.java

C:\herong>java EncodingAnalyzer2 US-ASCII
US-ASCII encoding:
00000000 > 00 - 0000007F > 7F
00000080 > 3F - 0010FFFF > 3F: Invalid range

Code Point > Byte Sequence - Code Point > Byte Sequence
```

The encoding map of US-ASCII is very simple:

- The encoded byte sequence is one byte only, taking the lower value byte of the code point.

- Valid code points only in the 0x0000 - 0x007F range.

- Note that the byte sequence of 0x3F, the "?" character, indicates an invalid character.

Here is the output of my sample program, EncodingAnalyzer2.java, for ISO-8859-1/ Latin 1 encoding with Java SE 7:

```
C:\herong>java EncodingAnalyzer2 ISO-8859-1
ISO-8859-1 encoding:
00000000 > 00 - 000000FF > FF
00000100 > 3F - 0010FFFF > 3F: Invalid range

Code Point > Byte Sequence - Code Point > Byte Sequence
```

The encoding map of ISO-8859-1/Latin 1 is also very simple:

- The encoded byte sequence is one byte only, taking the lower value byte of the code point.

- Valid code points only in the 0x0000 - 0x00FF range, full range of the lower value byte.

Character Set Encoding Maps - CP1252/Windows-1252

This section provides a tutorial example of analyzing and printing character set encoding maps for encoding: CP1252/Windows-1252, the default encoding for Java SE on Windows systems.

Here is the output of my sample program, EncodingAnalyzer2.java, for CP1252/Windows-1252 encoding with Java SE 7:

```
C:\herong>java EncodingAnalyzer2 CP1252
CP1252 encoding:
00000000 > 00 - 0000007F > 7F
00000080 > 3F - 0000009F > 3F: Invalid range
000000A0 > A0 - 000000FF > FF
00000100 > 3F - 00000151 > 3F: Invalid range
00000152 > 8C - 00000152 > 8C
00000153 > 9C - 00000153 > 9C
00000154 > 3F - 0000015F > 3F: Invalid range
00000160 > 8A - 00000160 > 8A
00000161 > 9A - 00000161 > 9A
00000162 > 3F - 00000177 > 3F: Invalid range
00000178 > 9F - 00000178 > 9F
00000179 > 3F - 0000017C > 3F: Invalid range
0000017D > 8E - 0000017D > 8E
0000017E > 9E - 0000017E > 9E
0000017F > 3F - 00000191 > 3F: Invalid range
00000192 > 83 - 00000192 > 83
00000193 > 3F - 000002C5 > 3F: Invalid range
000002C6 > 88 - 000002C6 > 88
000002C7 > 3F - 000002DB > 3F: Invalid range
000002DC > 98 - 000002DC > 98
000002DD > 3F - 00002012 > 3F: Invalid range
00002013 > 96 - 00002014 > 97
00002015 > 3F - 00002017 > 3F: Invalid range
00002018 > 91 - 00002019 > 92
0000201A > 82 - 0000201A > 82
```

```
0000201B > 3F - 0000201B > 3F: Invalid range
0000201C > 93 - 0000201D > 94
0000201E > 84 - 0000201E > 84
0000201F > 3F - 0000201F > 3F: Invalid range
00002020 > 86 - 00002021 > 87
00002022 > 95 - 00002022 > 95
00002023 > 3F - 00002025 > 3F: Invalid range
00002026 > 85 - 00002026 > 85
00002027 > 3F - 0000202F > 3F: Invalid range
00002030 > 89 - 00002030 > 89
00002031 > 3F - 00002038 > 3F: Invalid range
00002039 > 8B - 00002039 > 8B
0000203A > 9B - 0000203A > 9B
0000203B > 3F - 000020AB > 3F: Invalid range
000020AC > 80 - 000020AC > 80
000020AD > 3F - 00002121 > 3F: Invalid range
00002122 > 99 - 00002122 > 99
00002123 > 3F - 0010FFFF > 3F: Invalid range


Code Point > Byte Sequence - Code Point > Byte Sequence
```

The encoding map of CP1252/Windows-1252, which is the default encoding used by Java SE for Windows systems, is not so simple:

- The output sequence is always one byte.

- It is compatible with US-ASCII in the 0x0000 - 0x007F range.

- Only one section, 0x00A0 - 0x00FF, in the 0x0080 - 0x00FF range is valid.

- Only a small number of code points in the 0x0100 - 0xFFFF range is valid.

Character Set Encoding Maps - Unicode UTF-8

This section provides a tutorial example of analyzing and printing character set encoding maps for encoding: UTF-8 (Unicode Transformation Format - 8-bit), the most popular encoding for Unicode character set.

Here is the output of my sample program, EncodingAnalyzer2.java, for UTF-8 encoding
with Java SE 7:

```
C:\herong>java EncodingAnalyzer2 UTF-8
UTF-8 encoding:
00000000 > 00 - 0000007F > 7F
00000080 > C2 80 - 000000BF > C2 BF
000000C0 > C3 80 - 000000FF > C3 BF
00000100 > C4 80 - 0000013F > C4 BF
......
000007C0 > DF 80 - 000007FF > DF BF
00000800 > E0 A0 80 - 0000083F > E0 A0 BF
00000840 > E0 A1 80 - 0000087F > E0 A1 BF
00000880 > E0 A2 80 - 000008BF > E0 A2 BF
......
00000FC0 > E0 BF 80 - 00000FFF > E0 BF BF
00001000 > E1 80 80 - 0000103F > E1 80 BF
00001040 > E1 81 80 - 0000107F > E1 81 BF
00001080 > E1 82 80 - 000010BF > E1 82 BF
......
00001FC0 > E1 BF 80 - 00001FFF > E1 BF BF
00002000 > E2 80 80 - 0000203F > E2 80 BF
00002040 > E2 81 80 - 0000207F > E2 81 BF
00002080 > E2 82 80 - 000020BF > E2 82 BF
......
00002FC0 > E2 BF 80 - 00002FFF > E2 BF BF
00003000 > E3 80 80 - 0000303F > E3 80 BF
00003040 > E3 81 80 - 0000307F > E3 81 BF
00003080 > E3 82 80 - 000030BF > E3 82 BF
......
00003FC0 > E3 BF 80 - 00003FFF > E3 BF BF
00004000 > E4 80 80 - 0000403F > E4 80 BF
00004040 > E4 81 80 - 0000407F > E4 81 BF
00004080 > E4 82 80 - 000040BF > E4 82 BF
......
00004FC0 > E4 BF 80 - 00004FFF > E4 BF BF
00005000 > E5 80 80 - 0000503F > E5 80 BF
00005040 > E5 81 80 - 0000507F > E5 81 BF
```

```
00005080 > E5 82 80 - 000050BF > E5 82 BF

......

00005FC0 > E5 BF 80 - 00005FFF > E5 BF BF
00006000 > E6 80 80 - 0000603F > E6 80 BF
00006040 > E6 81 80 - 0000607F > E6 81 BF
00006080 > E6 82 80 - 000060BF > E6 82 BF

......

00006FC0 > E6 BF 80 - 00006FFF > E6 BF BF
00007000 > E7 80 80 - 0000703F > E7 80 BF
00007040 > E7 81 80 - 0000707F > E7 81 BF
00007080 > E7 82 80 - 000070BF > E7 82 BF

......

00007FC0 > E7 BF 80 - 00007FFF > E7 BF BF
00008000 > E8 80 80 - 0000803F > E8 80 BF
00008040 > E8 81 80 - 0000807F > E8 81 BF
00008080 > E8 82 80 - 000080BF > E8 82 BF

......

00008FC0 > E8 BF 80 - 00008FFF > E8 BF BF
00009000 > E9 80 80 - 0000903F > E9 80 BF
00009040 > E9 81 80 - 0000907F > E9 81 BF
00009080 > E9 82 80 - 000090BF > E9 82 BF

......

00009FC0 > E9 BF 80 - 00009FFF > E9 BF BF
0000A000 > EA 80 80 - 0000A03F > EA 80 BF
0000A040 > EA 81 80 - 0000A07F > EA 81 BF
0000A080 > EA 82 80 - 0000A0BF > EA 82 BF

......

0000AFC0 > EA BF 80 - 0000AFFF > EA BF BF
0000B000 > EB 80 80 - 0000B03F > EB 80 BF
0000B040 > EB 81 80 - 0000B07F > EB 81 BF
0000B080 > EB 82 80 - 0000B0BF > EB 82 BF

......

0000BFC0 > EB BF 80 - 0000BFFF > EB BF BF
0000C000 > EC 80 80 - 0000C03F > EC 80 BF
0000C040 > EC 81 80 - 0000C07F > EC 81 BF
0000C080 > EC 82 80 - 0000C0BF > EC 82 BF

......
```

```
0000CFC0 > EC BF 80 - 0000CFFF > EC BF BF

0000D000 > ED 80 80 - 0000D03F > ED 80 BF

0000D040 > ED 81 80 - 0000D07F > ED 81 BF

0000D080 > ED 82 80 - 0000D0BF > ED 82 BF

......

0000D7C0 > ED 9F 80 - 0000D7FF > ED 9F BF

0000D800 > 3F - 0000DFFF > 3F: Invalid range

0000E000 > EE 80 80 - 0000E03F > EE 80 BF

0000E040 > EE 81 80 - 0000E07F > EE 81 BF

0000E080 > EE 82 80 - 0000E0BF > EE 82 BF

......

0000EFC0 > EE BF 80 - 0000EFFF > EE BF BF

0000F000 > EF 80 80 - 0000F03F > EF 80 BF

0000F040 > EF 81 80 - 0000F07F > EF 81 BF

0000F080 > EF 82 80 - 0000F0BF > EF 82 BF

......

0000FFC0 > EF BF 80 - 0000FFFF > EF BF BF

00010000 > F0 90 80 80 - 0001003F > F0 90 80 BF

00010040 > F0 90 81 80 - 0001007F > F0 90 81 BF

00010080 > F0 90 82 80 - 000100BF > F0 90 82 BF

......

00020000 > F0 A0 80 80 - 0002003F > F0 A0 80 BF

00020040 > F0 A0 81 80 - 0002007F > F0 A0 81 BF

00020080 > F0 A0 82 80 - 000200BF > F0 A0 82 BF

......

0010FF40 > F4 8F BD 80 - 0010FF7F > F4 8F BD BF

0010FF80 > F4 8F BE 80 - 0010FFBF > F4 8F BE BF

0010FFC0 > F4 8F BF 80 - 0010FFFF > F4 8F BF BF


Code Point > Byte Sequence - Code Point > Byte Sequence
```

The encoding map of UTF-8, which is the most popular encodings used for the Unicode character set, is complex:

• The output sequence has variable number of bytes: from 1 byte to 4 bytes.

• It is backward compatible with US-ASCII encoding.

- One section of code points is not valid: 0xD800 - 0xDFFF. This invalid section is called the surrogate area, reserved for UTF-16 encoding use.

- As of Unicode 11.0, 0x10FFFF is highest valid character.

Character Set Encoding Maps - Unicode UTF-16, UTF-16BE, UTF-16LE

This section provides a tutorial example of analyzing and printing character set encoding maps for 3 encoding, UTF-16, UTF-16BE, and UTF-16LE, for Unicode character set.

Here is the output of my sample program, EncodingAnalyzer2.java, for UTF-16 encoding with Java SE 7:

```
C:\herong>java EncodingAnalyzer2 UTF-16

UTF-16 encoding:

00000000 > FE FF 00 00 - 000000FF > FE FF 00 FF

00000100 > FE FF 01 00 - 000001FF > FE FF 01 FF

00000200 > FE FF 02 00 - 000002FF > FE FF 02 FF

......

0000D700 > FE FF D7 00 - 0000D7FF > FE FF D7 FF

0000D800 > FE FF FF FD - 0000DFFF > FE FF FF FD (invalid range)

0000E000 > FE FF E0 00 - 0000E0FF > FE FF E0 FF

0000E100 > FE FF E1 00 - 0000E1FF > FE FF E1 FF

0000E200 > FE FF E2 00 - 0000E2FF > FE FF E2 FF

......

0000FF00 > FE FF FF 00 - 0000FFFF > FE FF FF FF

00010000 > FE FF D8 00 DC 00 - 000100FF > FE FF D8 00 DC FF

00010100 > FE FF D8 00 DD 00 - 000101FF > FE FF D8 00 DD FF

00010200 > FE FF D8 00 DE 00 - 000102FF > FE FF D8 00 DE FF

......

0010FF00 > FE FF DB FF DF 00 - 0010FFFF > FE FF DB FF DF FF


Code Point > Byte Sequence - Code Point > Byte Sequence
```

The encoding map of UTF-16, which is another encoding used for the Unicode character set, is much simpler than UTF-8:

- The output sequence is a variable length, 2 bytes or 4 bytes. Note that the leading 0xFEFF is the BOM (Byte Order Mark).

- It is not backward compatible with US-ASCII encoding.

- One section of code points is not valid: 0xD800 - 0xDFFF. The encoder generates a sequence of 0xFFFD for this range. This sequence represents the code point of the REPLACEMENT CHARACTER (U+FFFD) in Unicode.

Here is the output for UTF-16BE encoding, the big-endian variation of UTF-16 encoding:

```
C:\herong>java EncodingAnalyzer2 UTF-16BE
UTF-16BE encoding:
00000000 > 00 00 - 000000FF > 00 FF
00000100 > 01 00 - 000001FF > 01 FF
00000200 > 02 00 - 000002FF > 02 FF
......
0000D700 > D7 00 - 0000D7FF > D7 FF
0000D800 > FF FD - 0000DFFF > FF FD (invalid range)
0000E000 > E0 00 - 0000E0FF > E0 FF
0000E100 > E1 00 - 0000E1FF > E1 FF
0000E200 > E2 00 - 0000E2FF > E2 FF
......
0000FF00 > FF 00 - 0000FFFF > FF FF
00010000 > D8 00 DC 00 - 000100FF > D8 00 DC FF
00010100 > D8 00 DD 00 - 000101FF > D8 00 DD FF
00010200 > D8 00 DE 00 - 000102FF > D8 00 DE FF
......
0010FF00 > DB FF DF 00 - 0010FFFF > DB FF DF FF

Code Point > Byte Sequence - Code Point > Byte Sequence
```

The encoding map of UTF-16BE identical to UTF-16 except for the leading BOM 0xFEFF.

Here is the output for UTF-16LE encoding, the little-endian variation of UTF-16 encoding:

```
C:\herong>java EncodingAnalyzer2 UTF-16LE

UTF-16LE encoding:

00000000 > 00 00 - 0000D7FF > FF D7

0000D800 > FD FF - 0000DFFF > FD FF (invalid range)

0000E000 > 00 E0 - 0000FFFF > FF FF

00010000 > 00 D8 00 DC - 000103FF > 00 D8 FF DF

00010400 > 01 D8 00 DC - 000107FF > 01 D8 FF DF

00010800 > 02 D8 00 DC - 00010BFF > 02 D8 FF DF

......

0010FC00 > FF DB 00 DC - 0010FFFF > FF DB FF DF


Code Point > Byte Sequence - Code Point > Byte Sequence
```

The encoding map of UTF-16LE is identical to UTF-16BE except that the byte sequence
is reversed on each byte pair.

Character Set Encoding Maps - Unicode UTF-32, UTF-32BE, UTF-32LE

*This section provides a tutorial example of analyzing and printing character set encoding
maps for 3 encoding, UTF-32, UTF-32BE, and UTF-32LE, for Unicode character set.*

Here is the output of my sample program, EncodingAnalyzer2.java, for UTF-32
encoding with Java SE 7:

```
C:\herong>java EncodingAnalyzer2 UTF-32

UTF-32 encoding:

00000000 > 00 00 00 00 - 000000FF > 00 00 00 FF

00000100 > 00 00 01 00 - 000001FF > 00 00 01 FF

00000200 > 00 00 02 00 - 000002FF > 00 00 02 FF

......

0000D700 > 00 00 D7 00 - 0000D7FF > 00 00 D7 FF

0000D800 > 00 00 FF FD - 0000DFFF > 00 00 FF FD (invalid range)

0000E000 > 00 00 E0 00 - 0000E0FF > 00 00 E0 FF

0000E100 > 00 00 E1 00 - 0000E1FF > 00 00 E1 FF

0000E200 > 00 00 E2 00 - 0000E2FF > 00 00 E2 FF
```

```
. . . .
0010FF00 > 00 10 FF 00 - 0010FFFF > 00 10 FF FF
```

The encoding map of UTF-32, which is another encoding used for the Unicode character set, is the simplest encoding:

- The output sequence is a fixed length of 4 bytes.

- It is not backward compatible with US-ASCII encoding.

- Surprisingly, there is no leading BOM (Byte Order Mark) 0x0000FEFF in the output sequence!

Here is the output of my sample program, EncodingAnalyzer2.java, for UTF-32BE encoding with Java SE 7:

```
C:\herong>java EncodingAnalyzer2 UTF-32BE
UTF-32BE encoding:
00000000 > 00 00 00 00 - 000000FF > 00 00 00 FF
00000100 > 00 00 01 00 - 000001FF > 00 00 01 FF
00000200 > 00 00 02 00 - 000002FF > 00 00 02 FF
. . . . . .
0000D700 > 00 00 D7 00 - 0000D7FF > 00 00 D7 FF
0000D800 > 00 00 FF FD - 0000DFFF > 00 00 FF FD (invalid range)
0000E000 > 00 00 E0 00 - 0000E0FF > 00 00 E0 FF
0000E100 > 00 00 E1 00 - 0000E1FF > 00 00 E1 FF
0000E200 > 00 00 E2 00 - 0000E2FF > 00 00 E2 FF
. . . .
0010FF00 > 00 10 FF 00 - 0010FFFF > 00 10 FF FF
```

The output of UTF-32BE is identical to UTF-32.

Here is the output of my sample program, EncodingAnalyzer2.java, for UTF-32LE encoding with Java SE 7:

```
C:\herong>java EncodingAnalyzer2 UTF-32LE
UTF-32LE encoding:
00000000 > 00 00 00 00 - 0010FFFF > FF FF 10 00
```

Obviously, my sample program is not doing a good job on UTF-32LE. The last byte of the encode sequence never changes with UTF-32LE and my sample program uses the last byte to detect encoding pattern changes.

Exercise: Find a better way to print out encoding mapping tables.

Character Counter Program for Any Given Encoding

This section provides a tutorial example on how to write a simple program to count valid characters in a give encoding character set encoding.

As mentioned in the previous chapter, Java 11 supports 171 built-in character set encodings.

Of course, each encoding is designed for a specific character set only. As a simple exercise, I want to write a sample program that counts the number of characters in the character set of a given encoding.

The sample program, EncodingCounter2.java, counts the number of code points that are mapped valid byte sequences in the 0x0000 - 0x10FFFF range for a given encoding:

```
/* EncodingCounter2.java
 * Copyright (c) 2019 HerongYang.com. All Rights Reserved.
 */
import java.io.*;
import java.nio.*;
import java.nio.charset.*;
class EncodingCounter2 {
   static char hexDigit[] = {'0', '1', '2', '3', '4', '5', '6', '7',
                             '8', '9', 'A', 'B', 'C', 'D', 'E', 'F'};
   public static void main(String[] a) {
      String charset = "CP1252";
      if (a.length>0) charset = a[0];
      System.out.println(charset+" encoding:");
      int lastByte = 0;
      int lastLength = 0;
      byte[] startSequence = null;
      int startChar = 0;
      byte[] endSequence = null;
      int endChar = 0;
```

```
   boolean isFirstChar = true;
int validCount = 0;
int subCount = 0;
int totalCount = 0x00110000;
for (int i=0; i<totalCount; i++) {
   subCount++;
   int c = i;
   byte[] b = encodeByEncoder(c,charset);
   int l = 0;
   int lb = 0;
   if (b!=null) {
      l = b.length;
      lb = ((int) b[l-1]) & 0x00FF;
      validCount++;
   }
   if (isFirstChar==true) {
      isFirstChar = false;
      startSequence = b;
      startChar = c;
      lastByte = lb - 1;
      lastLength = l;
   }
   if (!(l==lastLength)) {
      System.out.print(intToHex(startChar)+" >");
      printBytes(startSequence);
      System.out.print(" - "+intToHex(endChar)+" >");
      printBytes(endSequence);
      System.out.println(" = "+(subCount-1));
      startSequence = b;
      startChar = c;
      subCount = 1;
   }
   endSequence = b;
   endChar = c;
   lastLength = l;
   lastByte = lb;
}
```

```
      System.out.print(intToHex(startChar)+" >");
      printBytes(startSequence);
      System.out.print(" - "+intToHex(endChar)+" >");
      printBytes(endSequence);
      System.out.println(" = "+(subCount));
      System.out.println("Total characters = "+totalCount);
      System.out.println("Valid characters = "+validCount);
      System.out.println("Invalid characters = "
         +(totalCount-validCount));
   }
   public static byte[] encodeByEncoder(int c, String cs) {
      Charset cso = null;
      byte[] b = null;
      try {
         cso = Charset.forName(cs);
         CharsetEncoder e =  cso.newEncoder();
         e.reset();
         ByteBuffer bb
            = e.encode(CharBuffer.wrap(Character.toChars(c)));
         if (bb.limit()>0) b = copyBytes(bb.array(),bb.limit());
      } catch (IllegalCharsetNameException e) {
         System.out.println(e.toString());
      } catch (CharacterCodingException e) {
         // invalid character, return null
      }
      return b;
   }
   public static void printBytes(byte[] b) {
      if (b!=null) {
         for (int j=0; j<b.length; j++)
            System.out.print(" "+byteToHex(b[j]));
      } else {
         System.out.print(" XX");
      }
   }
   public static byte[] copyBytes(byte[] a, int l) {
      byte[] b = new byte[l];
```

```
      for (int i=0; i<Math.min(1,a.length); i++) b[i] = a[i];
      return b;
   }
   public static String byteToHex(byte b) {
      char[] a = { hexDigit[(b >> 4) & 0x0f], hexDigit[b & 0x0f] };
      return new String(a);
   }
   public static String charToHex(char c) {
      byte hi = (byte) (c >>> 8);
      byte lo = (byte) (c & 0xff);
      return byteToHex(hi) + byteToHex(lo);
   }
   public static String intToHex(int i) {
      char hi = (char) (i >>> 16);
      char lo = (char) (i & 0xffff);
      return charToHex(hi) + charToHex(lo);
   }
}
```

Note that:

- CharsetEncoder.encode() is used to encode the code point stored as "int" type.

- The encoding name should be specified as the command line argument.

The output of this program will be discussed in the next section.

Character Set Encoding Comparison

This section provides a tutorial example on how to compare some commonly used character set encodings in number of characters, byte sequence sizes and ASCII compatibilities.

Here is the output of my sample program, EncodingCounter2.java, for US-ASCII encoding:

```
C:\herong>javac EncodingCounter2.java
```

```
C:\herong>java EncodingCounter2 US-ASCII
US-ASCII encoding:
00000000 > 00 - 0000007F > 7F = 128
00000080 > XX - 000FFFFF > XX = 1048448
Total characters = 1048576
Valid characters = 128
Invalid characters = 1048448
```

This tells us that the US-ASCII character set has only 128 characters.

Run EncodingCounter.java again with ISO-8859-1 (Latin 1) as argument, you will get:

```
C:\herong>java EncodingCounter2 ISO-8859-1
ISO-8859-1 encoding:
00000000 > 00 - 000000FF > FF = 256
00000100 > XX - 000FFFFF > XX = 1048320
Total characters = 1048576
Valid characters = 256
Invalid characters = 1048320
```

This tells us that the ISO-8859-1 character set has only 256 characters.

The following table is based on the output of the EncodingCouter.java program. It provides a brief comparison between the some commonly used encodings:

Encoding Name	Map Size	US-ASCII Compatible	Notes
US-ASCII	128	Y	7-bit characters only
ISO-8859-1	256	Y	8-bit (single byte) characters
CP1252	251	Y	One byte output, with code points up to 0x2122
UTF-8	1046528	Y	1-4 bytes, complex algorithm
UTF-16BE	1046528	N	2-4 bytes, code point and surrogate pairs
UTF-16LE	1046528	N	2-4 bytes, reversing byte pair of UTF-16BE
UTF-16	1046528	N	4-6 bytes, same as UTF-16BE with leading BOM
UTF-32BE	1046528	N	4 bytes, code point
UTF-32LE	1046528	N	4 bytes, reversing byte sequence of UTF-32BE
UTF-32	1046528	N	4 bytes, same as UTF-32BE
GB2312	7573	Y	1-2 bytes, Chinese 1980 standard
GBK	24068	Y	1-2 bytes, Chinese 1993 standard

GB18030	1046528	Y	1-4 bytes, superset of GBK, 2000 standard
BIG5	13831	Y	1-2 bytes, traditional Chinese character set

Encoding Conversion Programs for Encoded Text Files

This chapter provides tutorial notes and example codes on character encoding conversion. Topics include entering Unicode characters with \uxxxx escape sequences; viewing encoded text files in Hex values; converting text files from one encoding to another; viewing encoded text files in Web browsers; viewing Unicode signs/symbols in different encodings.

Conclusion:

- Java program seems to be a good way of storing Unicode characters into a file, if you don't have any good text editor that handles Unicode characters.

- When converting text file from one encoding to another, you need to make sure that all characters in the text file are valid characters in the character set of the output encoding.

- IE is a very good tool to view Unicode text, if you installed all the required fonts.

Exercise: Adding more messages in other languages in UnicodeHello.java.

\uxxxx - Entering Unicode Data in Java Programs

This section provides a tutorial example on how to enter Unicode characters using \uxxxx escape sequences in a Java program, and same them to any giving character set encoding.

Encoding conversion is about reading strings of characters stored in a file encoded with encoding A, and writing them into another file encoded with encoding B.

Before going into details on encoding conversion, let's talk briefly about Unicode data entry. How do we enter Unicode characters into a file? There are a couple of ways to do that:

- Using encoding specific word processors. Usually, one word processor will allow you to enter characters of a particular language or encoding.

- Using Hex editors to enter directly the byte sequences representing the desired characters in a specific encoding.

- Using Unicode based programming language to enter the desired characters as string literals.

Word processors are too specific to be discussed here.

Hex editors are ultimate data entry tools for Unicode characters. They can also be used to inspect and repair encoded text files. But Hex editors are very hard to use. Note that Notepad on Windows is not a Hex editor. But UltraEdit on Windows is a Hex editor.

Using Unicode based programming language, like Java, to enter Unicode characters into a file is very interesting. For each character in a string literal, you can use the \uxxxx escape sequence to represent the character by enter its code point value in Hex format.

Here is a sample program, UnicodeHello.java, showing you how to use \uxxxx escape sequences:

```
/* UnicodeHello.java
 * Copyright (c) 2019 HerongYang.com. All Rights Reserved.
 *
 * This program is a simple tool to allow you to enter several lines of
 * text, and write them into a file using the specified encoding
 * (charset name). The input text lines uses Java string convention,
 * which allows you to enter ASCII characters directly, and any non
 * ASCII characters with escape sequences.
 *
 * This version of the program is to write out the "Hello world!"
 * message in some different languages.
 */
```

```
import java.io.*;
class UnicodeHello {
    public static void main(String[] a) {
        // The following Array contains text to be saved into the output
        // File. To enter your own text, just replace this Array.
        String[] text = {
"Hello computer! - English", // ASCII
"\u7535\u8111\u4F60\u597D\uFF01 - Simplified Chinese", // GB2312
"\u96FB\u8166\u4F60\u597D\uFE57 - Traditional Chinese" // Big5
        };
        String outFile = "hello.utf-16be";
        if (a.length>0) outFile = a[0];
        String outCharsetName = "utf-16be";
        if (a.length>1) outCharsetName = a[1];
        String crlf = System.getProperty("line.separator");
        try {
            OutputStreamWriter out = new OutputStreamWriter(
                new FileOutputStream(outFile), outCharsetName);
            for (int i=0; i<text.length; i++) {
                out.write(text[i]);
                out.write(crlf);
            }
            out.close();
        } catch (IOException e) {
            System.out.println(e.toString());
        }
    }
}
```

As you can see from the source code, this program will write the "Hello computer!" message in several languages. Let's compile this program and run it to get the characters saved into a file with UTF-16BE encoding:

```
C:\herong>javac UnicodeHello.java


C:\herong>java UnicodeHello hello.utf-16be utf-16be
```

Now we have a text file with characters saved in UTF-16BE encoding. Read the next section on how to view and inspect this UTF-16BE encoded file.

HexWriter.java - Converting Encoded Byte Sequences to Hex Values

This section provides a tutorial example on how to write a sample program, HexWriter.java, to convert encoded byte sequences to Hex values to help viewing encoded text files.

By running the sample program, UnicodeHello.java, presented in the previous section, I got this text file saved in UTF-16BE encoding, hello.utf-16be. The next question is how can I view and inspect this UTF-16BE encoded file. Normal text editors will not able to show the content of this correctly.

I have two choices: using a Hex editor to open the file or convert the file to Hex value file with a program.

I decide to write a simple Java program convert UTF-16BE byte sequences into Hex decimal digits to allow me inspecting the code values of the saved characters. Remember UTF-16BE encoding breaks the code values into two bytes directly without any changes in the value. Here is a program to convert any data file into Hex decimal digits:

```java
/* HexWriter.java
 * Copyright (c) 2019 HerongYang.com. All Rights Reserved.
 * This program allows you to convert and data file to a new data
 * in Hex format with 16 bytes (32 Hex digits) per line.
 */
import java.io.*;
class HexWriter {
    static char hexDigit[] = {'0', '1', '2', '3', '4', '5', '6', '7',
                              '8', '9', 'A', 'B', 'C', 'D', 'E', 'F'};
    public static void main(String[] a) {
        String inFile = a[0];
        String outFile = a[1];
        int bufSize = 16;
        byte[] buffer = new byte[bufSize];
```

```
        String crlf = System.getProperty("line.separator");
        try {
            FileInputStream in = new FileInputStream(inFile);
            OutputStreamWriter out = new OutputStreamWriter(
                new FileOutputStream(outFile));
            int n = in.read(buffer,0,bufSize);
    String s = null;
            int count = 0;
            while (n!=-1) {
                count += n;
                s = bytesToHex(buffer,0,n);
                out.write(s);
                out.write(crlf);
                n = in.read(buffer,0,bufSize);
            }
            in.close();
            out.close();
            System.out.println("Number of input bytes: "+count);
        } catch (IOException e) {
            System.out.println(e.toString());
        }
    }
    public static String bytesToHex(byte[] b, int off, int len) {
        StringBuffer buf = new StringBuffer();
        for (int j=0; j<len; j++)
            buf.append(byteToHex(b[off+j]));
        return buf.toString();
    }
    public static String byteToHex(byte b) {
        char[] a = { hexDigit[(b >> 4) & 0x0f], hexDigit[b & 0x0f] };
        return new String(a);
    }
}
```

Compile this program and run it to convert hello.utf-16be:

```
C:\herong>javac HexWriter.java
```

```
C:\herong>java java HexWriter hello.utf-16be hello.hex
```

Okay, here is the content of hello.hex:

```
00480065006C006C006F00200063006F
006D0070007500740065007200210020
002D00200045006E0067006C00690073
0068000D000A753581114F60597DFF01
0020002D002000530069006D0070006C
00690066006900650064002000430068
0069006E006500730065000D000A96FB
81664F60597DFE570020002D00200054
00720061006400690074006900 6F006E
0061006C002000430068006900 6E0065
00730065000D000A
```

If you know how to read Hex number, you should be able to see:

- "00480065006C006C006F" represents "Hello" in UTF-16BE encoding.
- "753581114F60597DFF01" represents the Simplified Chinese message in UTF-16BE encoding.
- "96FB81664F60597DFE57" represents the Traditional Chinese message in UTF-16BE encoding.

Remember to use line break sequence 000D000A (\r\n) to help finding the first character of each line.

EncodingConverter.java - Encoding Conversion Sample Program

This section provides a tutorial example on how to write a sample program, EncodingConverter.java, to convert text files from one character set encoding to another.

With the help of HexWriter.java, I know that file hello.utf-16be stores strings of characters in UTF-16BE encoding.

Now I want to write a sample program, EncodingConverter.java, to convert text files from one character set encoding to another:

```
/* EncodingConverter.java
 * Copyright (c) 2019 HerongYang.com. All Rights Reserved.
 *
 * This program allows you to convert a text file in one encoding
 * to another file in a different encoding.
 */
import java.io.*;
class EncodingConverter {
   public static void main(String[] a) {
      String inFile = a[0];
      String inCharsetName = a[1];
      String outFile = a[2];
      String outCharsetName = a[3];
      try {
         InputStreamReader in = new InputStreamReader(
            new FileInputStream(inFile), inCharsetName);
         OutputStreamWriter out = new OutputStreamWriter(
            new FileOutputStream(outFile), outCharsetName);
         int c = in.read();
         int n = 0;
         while (c!=-1) {
            out.write(c);
            n++;
            c = in.read();
         }
         in.close();
         out.close();
         System.out.println("Number of characters: "+n);
         System.out.println("Number of input bytes: "
            +(new File(inFile)).length());
         System.out.println("Number of output bytes: "
            +(new File(outFile)).length());
      } catch (IOException e) {
         System.out.println(e.toString());
      }
```

```
   }
}
```

Compile this program and use it to convert our hello message file into several encodings:

```
C:\herong>javac EncodingConverter.java

C:\herong>java EncodingConverter hello.utf-16be utf-16be \
   hello.ascii ascii
Number of characters: 84
Number of input bytes: 168
Number of output bytes: 84

C:\herong>java EncodingConverter hello.utf-16be utf-16be \
   hello.iso-8859-1 iso-8859-1
Number of characters: 84
Number of input bytes: 168
Number of output bytes: 94

C:\herong>java EncodingConverter hello.utf-16be utf-16be \
   hello.utf-8 utf-8
Number of characters: 84
Number of input bytes: 168
Number of output bytes: 104

C:\herong>java EncodingConverter hello.utf-16be utf-16be \
   hello.gbk gbk
Number of characters: 84
Number of input bytes: 168
Number of output bytes: 94

C:\herong>java EncodingConverter hello.utf-16be utf-16be \
   hello.big5 big5
Number of characters: 84
Number of input bytes: 168
Number of output bytes: 92
```

```
C:\herong>java EncodingConverter hello.utf-16be utf-16be
   hello.shift_jis shift_jis
Number of characters: 84
Number of input bytes: 168
Number of output bytes: 89
```

By reviewing output files, you should see that:

hello.ascii - In this file, only the English message is good, because it contains only ASCII characters. Both Simplified Chinese and Traditional Chinese messages are not good. Characters in these messages are replaced by 0x3F, an indication of invalid code.

hello.iso-8859-1 - This is identical to hello.ascii, because there is no characters in the 0x80 - 0xFF range.

hello.utf-8 - This file contains all messages with no damages. The ASCII characters are stored as one-byte characters as expected.

hello.gbk - In this file, the Simplified Chinese message is good. In fact, characters in the Simplified Chinese message are stored as code values in GBK character set standard. The English message is also good, because GBK is ASCII backward compatible. We are lucky with the Traditional Chinese message, because the Big5 characters used in the message are also valid in GBK standard. If you use some Big5 special characters, the result could be different.

hello.big5 - In this file, the Traditional Chinese message is good. In fact, characters in the Traditional Chinese message are stored as code values in Big5 character set standard. The English message is also good, because Big5 is ASCII backward compatible. We are not lucky with the Simplified Chinese message, two GB characters used in the message are not valid in Big5 standard. 0x3F was stored for those characters.

hello.shift_jis - In this file, the English message is still good. Some of the characters from both Simplified and Traditional Chinese messages are invalid, replaced by 0x3F placeholders. Some of the Chinese characters are still valid in Shift_JIS character set. This is not so surprising, because there are many shared characters in Chinese and Japanese.

Viewing Encoded Text Files in Web Browsers

This section provides a tutorial example on how to view text files with different encodings with Web browser Internet Explorer. The encoded text file should be modified to add proper HTML tags using the sample program EncodingHtml.java.

Now, we have our greeting messages saved in many different encodings. The next question is how do display them as glyph of the corresponding languages on the screen. One of the ways I have used in the past is to run a multi-language enabled Web browser like IE to view the text files. To do this, we have to mark up the text into a html file, by using a program like this one:

```
/* EncodingHtml.java
 * Copyright (c) 2019 HerongYang.com. All Rights Reserved.
 *
 * This program allows you to mark up a text file into an HTML file.
 */
import java.io.*;
import java.util.*;
class EncodingHtml {
    static HashMap charsetMap = new HashMap();
    public static void main(String[] a) {
        String inFile = a[0];
        String inCharsetName = a[1];
        String outFile = inFile + ".html";
        try {
            InputStreamReader in = new InputStreamReader(
                new FileInputStream(inFile), inCharsetName);
            OutputStreamWriter out = new OutputStreamWriter(
                new FileOutputStream(outFile), inCharsetName);
            writeHead(out, inCharsetName);
            int c = in.read();
            int n = 0;
            while (c!=-1) {
                out.write(c);
                n++;
```

```
              c = in.read();
          }
          writeTail(out);
          in.close();
          out.close();
          System.out.println("Number of characters: "+n);
       } catch (IOException e) {
          System.out.println(e.toString());
       }
   }
   public static void writeHead(OutputStreamWriter out, String cs)
       throws IOException {
       out.write("<html><head>\n");
       out.write("<meta http-equiv=\"Content-Type\""+
          " content=\"text/html; charset="+cs+"\">\n");
       out.write("</head><body><pre>");
   }
   public static void writeTail(OutputStreamWriter out)
       throws IOException {
       out.write("</pre></body></html>\n");
   }
}
```

Now, let's compile this program and run it with hello.utf-8:

```
C:\herong>javac EncodingHtml.java


C:\herong>java EncodingHtml hello.utf-8 utf-8
Number of characters: 84
```

If you have installed IE with the Chinese language support, you should be able to open the output file, hello.utf-8.html, and enjoy reading the messages in English, Simplified Chinese, and Traditional Chinese.

Then, run EncodingHtml.java with other encodings,

```
C:\herong>java EncodingHtml hello.gbk gbk
Number of characters: 84
```

```
C:\herong>java EncodingHtml hello.big5 big5
Number of characters: 84


C:\herong>java EncodingHtml hello.shift_jis shift_jis
Number of characters: 84
```

View the output files with a Web browser, and compare the results:

- hello.utf-8.html - Browser sets View/Encoding to utf-8. All messages are perfect.

- hello.gbk.html - Browser sets View/Encoding to gb2312. All messages are perfect.

- hello.big5.html - Browser sets View/Encoding to big5. Simplified Chinese message has two bad characters.

- hello.shift_jis - Browser sets View/Encoding to shift_jis. Both Simplified and Traditional Chinese messages have bad characters.

If you manually change the setting of View/Encoding, IE will not be able to show the message with the right glyph.

Unicode Signs in Different Encodings

This section provides a tutorial example on how to write sample programs to create some Unicode signs in various encodings and view them in a Web browser.

I wanted to play with my utility programs mentioned in this chapter one more time with some Unicode signs. So I copied UnicodeHello.java and created UnicodeSign.java:

```
/* UnicodeSign.java
 * Copyright (c) 2019 HerongYang.com. All Rights Reserved.
 *
 * This program is a simple tool to allow you to enter several lines of
 * text, and write them into a file using the specified encoding
 * (charset name). The input text lines uses Java string convention,
 * which allows you to enter ASCII characters directly, and any non
 * ASCII characters with escape sequences.
 *
 * This version of the program is to write out some interesting signs.
```

```
 */
import java.io.*;
class UnicodeSign {
   public static void main(String[] a) {
      // The following Array contains text to be saved into the output
      // File. To enter your own text, just replace this Array.
      String[] text = {
"U+005C(\\)REVERSE SOLIDUS", //\u005C is '\', cannot be entered directly
"U+007E(\u007E)TILDE",
"U+00A2(\u00A2)CENT SIGN",
"U+00A3(\u00A3)POUND SING",
"U+00A5(\u00A5)YEN SIGN",
"U+00A6(\u00A6)BROKEN BAR",
"U+00A7(\u00A7)SECTION SIGN",
"U+00A9(\u00A9)COPYRIGHT SIGN",
"U+00AC(\u00AC)NOT SIGN",
"U+00AE(\u00AE)REGISTERED SIGN",
"U+2022(\u2022)BULLET",
"U+2023(\u2023)TRIANGULAR BULLET",
"U+203B(\u203B)REFERENCE MARK",
"U+2043(\u2043)HYPHEN BULLET",
"U+FF04(\uFF04)FULLWIDTH DOLLAR SIGN",
"U+FF05(\uFF05)FULLWIDTH PERCENT SIGN",
"U+FF08(\uFF08)FULLWIDTH LEFT PARENTHESIS",
"U+FF09(\uFF09)FULLWIDTH RIGHT PARENTHESIS",
"U+FF10(\uFF10)FULLWIDTH DIGIT ZERO",
"U+FF11(\uFF11)FULLWIDTH DIGIT ONE",
"U+FF21(\uFF21)FULLWIDTH LATIN CAPITAL LETTER A",
"U+FF22(\uFF22)FULLWIDTH LATIN CAPITAL LETTER B",
"U+FF41(\uFF41)FULLWIDTH LATIN SMALL LETTER A",
"U+FF42(\uFF42)FULLWIDTH LATIN SMALL LETTER B",
"U+FFE0(\uFFE0)FULLWIDTH CENT SIGN",
"U+FFE1(\uFFE1)FULLWIDTH POND SIGN",
"U+FFE5(\uFFE5)FULLWIDTH YEN SIGN"
      };
      String outFile = "sign.utf-16be";
      if (a.length>0) outFile = a[0];
```

```
        String outCharsetName = "utf-16be";
        if (a.length>1) outCharsetName = a[1];
        String crlf = System.getProperty("line.separator");
        try {
            OutputStreamWriter out = new OutputStreamWriter(
                new FileOutputStream(outFile), outCharsetName);
            for (int i=0; i<text.length; i++) {
                out.write(text[i]);
                out.write(crlf);
            }
            out.close();
        } catch (IOException e) {
            System.out.println(e.toString());
        }
    }
}
```

Then I ran this program, and converted the output file with different encodings:

```
javac UnicodeSign.java
java UnicodeSign sign.utf-16be utf-16be
java EncodingConverter sign.utf-16be utf-16be sign.utf-8 utf-8
java EncodingHtml sign.utf-8 utf-8
java EncodingConverter sign.utf-16be utf-16be sign.gbk gbk
java EncodingHtml sign.gbk gbk
java EncodingConverter sign.utf-16be utf-16be sign.shift_jis shift_jis
java EncodingHtml sign.shif_jis shift_jis
java EncodingConverter sign.utf-16be utf-16be sign.johab johab
java EncodingHtml sign.johab johab
```

Then I viewed the different encoded test files with IE, and noticed that:

- sign.utf-8.html - The signs looked very good except two: TRIANGULAR BULLET and DASH BULLET.

- sign.gbk.html - Many low-code-point signs were wrong, like CENT SIGN.

- sign.shift_jis.html - Some signs were wrong, like FULLWIDTH CENT SIGN, but CENT SIGN is correct.

- sign.johab.html - Like the gbk encoding, many low-code-point signs were wrong, like CENT SIGN.

Using Notepad as a Unicode Text Editor

This chapter provides notes and tutorial examples on using Nodepad as a Unicode text editor. Topics including opening Unicode text files in 3 encodings: UTF-8, UTF-16BE, and UTF-16LE; saving and opening Unicode text files with the BOM character.

Conclusions:

- Notepad can be used to edit Unicode text files.

- Notepad allows you to save Unicode text files in UTF-8 encoding. But it prepends the BOM (Byte Order Mark) character to file. This is unnecessary.

- Notepad allows you to save Unicode text files in UTF-16 encoding in 2 formats: Big-Endian with BOM and Little-Endian with BOM.

- Notepad can open Unicode text files in UTF-8 and UTF-16LE encodings without the BOM character.

- Notepad can not open Unicode text files in UTF-16BE encoding format correctly.

- The BOM character is the "ZERO WIDTH NO-BREAK SPACE" character, U+FEFF, in the Unicode character set.

What Is Notepad

This section provides a quick introduction of the default text editor, Notepad, included in Windows system. Notepad does support Unicode text files.

What Is Notepad? Notepad is text file editor included in Windows systems. The Help > Help Topics menu of the Notepad version on my Windows system gives me the following overview of Notepad:

Notepad is a basic text editor that you can use to create simple documents. The most common use for Notepad is to view or edit text (.txt) files, but many users find Notepad a simple tool for creating Web pages.

Because Notepad supports only very basic formatting, you cannot accidentally save special formatting in documents that need to remain pure text. This is especially useful when creating HTML documents for a Web page because special characters or other formatting may not appear in your published Web page or may even cause errors.

You can save your Notepad files as Unicode, ANSI, UTF-8, or big-endian Unicode. These formats provide you greater flexibility when working with documents that use different character sets.

Opening UTF-8 Text Files

This section provides a tutorial example on how to open a UTF-8 text file with Nodepad correctly by selecting the UTF-8 encoding option on the open file dialog box.

According to the Notepad help information, Notepad support 3 Unicode encodings: Unicode, UTF-8, and big-endian Unicode. Let's try to use Notepad to open the UTF-8 text file, hello.utf-8, created from the previous chapter first.

1. Run Notepad and click menu File > Open. The open file dialog box comes up.

2. Select the hello.utf-8 text file and select the UTF-8 option in the Encoding field. See the picture below:

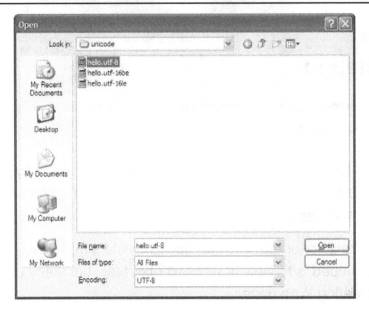

Notepad Open UTF-8 File

3. Click the Open button. The UTF-8 file opens in the editor correctly. See the picture below:

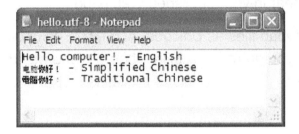

Notepad Edit UTF-8 File

Very nice. This proves that Notepad can open UTF-8 text file correctly if the UTF-8 encoding option is selected.

If you select a different encoding, like Unicode, the UTF-8 text file will be opened incorrectly. Try it out yourself.

Opening UTF-16BE Text Files

This section provides a tutorial example on how to open a UTF-16BE text file with Nodepad. But Notepad failed to open correctly the UTF-16BE text created by myself.

Now let's try to use Notepad to open the UTF-16BE text file, hello.utf-16be, created from the previous chapter.

1. Run Notepad and click menu File > Open. The open file dialog box comes up.

2. Select the hello.utf-16be text file and select the "Unicode big endian" option in the Encoding field. See the picture below:

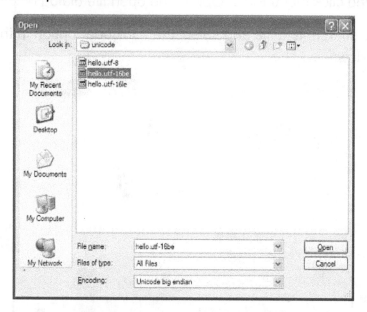

Notepad Open UTF-16BE File

3. Click the Open button. The UTF-16BE file opens in the editor incorrectly. See the picture below:

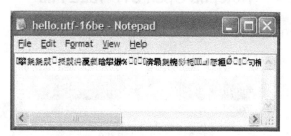

Notepad Edit UTF-16BE File

Very bad. This proves that Notepad can not open UTF-16BE text file created by myself.

Opening UTF-16LE Text Files

This section provides a tutorial example on how to open a UTF-16LE text file with Nodepad correctly by selecting the Unicode encoding option on the open file dialog box.

In the next test, I want to use Notepad to open the UTF-16LE text file, hello.utf-16le, created from the previous chapter.

1. Run Notepad and click menu File > Open. The open file dialog box comes up.

2. Select the hello.utf-16le text file and select the "Unicode" option in the Encoding field. See the picture below:

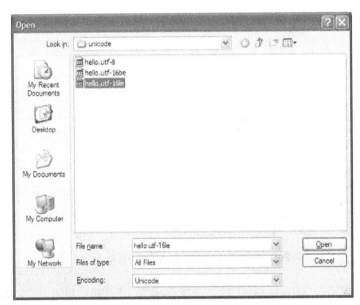

Notepad Open UTF-16LE File

3. Click the Open button. The UTF-16LE file opens in the editor correctly. See the picture below:

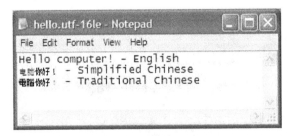

Notepad Edit UTF-16LE File

Very nice. This proves that Notepad can open UTF-16LE text file correctly if the Unicode encoding option is selected. This also tells us that Notepad's Unicode encoding means UTF-16LE encoding.

If you select a different encoding, like UTF-8, the UTF-16LE text file will be opened incorrectly. Try it out yourself.

Saving Files in UTF-8 Option

This section provides a tutorial example on how to save text files with Nodepad by selecting the UTF-8 encoding option on the save file dialog box.

After testing the Notepad open function, now I want to test the save function with the UTF-8 encoding.

1. Run Notepad and open hello.utf-8 correctly with the UTF-8 encoding option selected.

2. Click the File > "Save As" menu. The "Save As" dialog box comes up.

3. Enter notepad_utf-8 as the new file name and select UTF-8 option in the Encoding field.

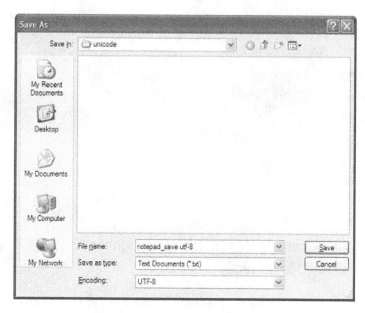

Notepad Save UTF-8 File

4. Click the Save button. Notepad saves the text to a new file named as: notepad_utf-8.txt.

5. To see how my text is saved by Notepad, I need to run my HEX dump program on notepad_utf-8.txt:

```
C:\herong\unicode>java HexWriter notepad_utf-8.txt notepad_utf-8.hex
Number of input bytes: 107

C:\herong\unicode>type notepad_utf-8.hex
EFBBBF48656C6C6F20636F6D70757465
7221202D20456E676C6973680D0AE794
B5E88491E4BDA0E5A5BDEFBC81202D20
53696D706C6966696564204368696E65
73650D0AE99BBBE885A6E4BDA0E5A5BD
EFB997202D2054726164974696F6E61
6C204368696E6573650D0A
```

5. To compare the UTF-8 text file created by Notepad with my original UTF-8 file, I need to run my HEX dump program on hello.utf-8:

```
C:\herong\unicode>java HexWriter hello.utf-8 hello_utf-8.hex
Number of input bytes: 104

C:\herong\unicode>type hello_utf-8.hex
48656C6C6F20636F6D70757465722120
2D20456E676C6973680D0AE794B5E884
91E4BDA0E5A5BDEFBC81202D2053696D
706C6966696564204368696E6573650D
0AE99BBBE885A6E4BDA0E5A5BDEFB997
202D2054726164974696F6E616C2043
68696E6573650D0A
```

The UTF-8 text file saved by Notepad is identical to my original UTF-8 text file except for those 3 bytes in the beginning, "EFBBBF". If we ignore "EFBBBF", we can say that Notepad saves UTF-8 text file correctly.

So what is this "EFBBBF" and why it is added? See the next section for a brief explanation.

Byte Order Mark (BOM) - FEFF - EFBBBF

This section provides a brief introduction on the Byte Order Mark (BOM) character, U+FEFF, used as the Unicode character stream signature when prepended to a character stream. The U+FEFF character becomes a 3-byte sequence of EFBBBF when encoded in UTF-8.

What Is BOM (Byte Order Mark)? BOM is the informal name of the special Unicode character U+FEFF "ZERO WIDTH NO-BREAK SPACE", when it is used to prepend to a stream of Unicode characters as a "signature". This signature tells the receiver of this stream to be ready to process Unicode characters and pay attention to the serialization order of the encoding octets.

When this BOM character, U+FEFF, is serialized in UTF-8 encoding, it becomes an octet sequence of EF BB BF (\xEFBBBF).

As you can see from the previous tutorial, Notepad prepends U+FEFF to the text and converted it to EFBBBF when saving the text in UTF-8 encoding. This is why I was getting these 3 extra bytes, EFBBBF, at the beginning of the saved UTF-8 text file.

With the introduction of the BOM character, now we need to ready to support two variations of UTF-8 text file formats:

- UTF-8 text file with no leading BOM character.

- UTF-8 text file with the leading BOM character.

Read RFC 3629, "UTF-8, a transformation format of ISO 10646", November 2003 at http://tools.ietf.org/html/rfc3629 for more information.

Prepending the BOM character to Unicode text files is recommended by RFC 3629.

Saving Files in "Unicode Big Endian" Option

This section provides a tutorial example on how to save text files with Nodepad by selecting the 'Unicode big endian' encoding option on the save file dialog box.

In the next test, I want to try the save function with the "Unicode big endian" encoding.

1. Run Notepad and open hello.utf-8 correctly with the UTF-8 encoding option selected.

2. Click the File > "Save As" menu. The "Save As" dialog box comes up.

3. Enter notepad_utf-16be as the new file name and select "Unicode big endian" option in the Encoding field.

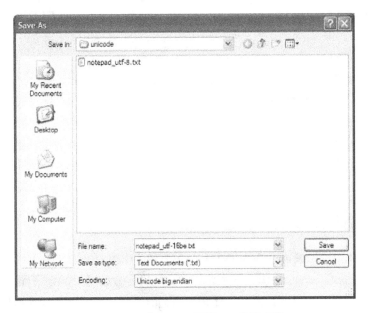

Notepad Save UTF-16BE File

4. Click the Save button. Notepad saves the text to a new file named as: notepad_utf-16be.txt.

5. To see how my text is saved by Notepad, I need to run my HEX dump program on notepad_utf-16be.txt:

```
C:\herong\unicode>java HexWriter notepad_utf-16be.txt
    notepad_utf-16be.hex


Number of input bytes: 170


C:\herong\unicode>type notepad_utf-16be.hex
FEFF00480065006C006C006F00200063
006F006D0070007500740065007200210
0020002D00200045006E0067006C0069
00730068000D000A753581114F60597D
FF010020002D002000530069006D0070
006C006900660069006500640020004 3
00680069006E00650073006500 0D000A
96FB81664F60597DFE570020002D0020
00540072006100640069007400690 06F
```

```
006E0061006C0020004300680069006E
006500730065000D000A
```

Very nice. This is a perfect UTF-16 encoding file using the Big-Endian with BOM format. Those leading 2 bytes represent the BOM flag, which is not part of the text.

Conclusion - The "Unicode big endian" encoding option of Notepad matches the "Big-Endian with BOM" format of Unicode UTF-16 encoding.

Saving Files in "Unicode" Option

This section provides a tutorial example on how to save text files with Nodepad by selecting the Unicode encoding option on the save file dialog box.

In the next test, I want to try the save function with the Unicode encoding.

1. Run Notepad and open hello.utf-8 correctly with the UTF-8 encoding option selected.

2. Click the File > "Save As" menu. The "Save As" dialog box comes up.

3. Enter notepad_utf-16le as the new file name and select "Unicode" option in the Encoding field.

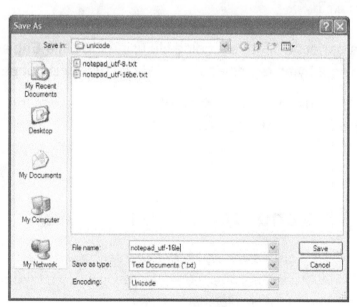

Notepad Save UTF-16LE File

4. Click the Save button. Notepad saves the text to a new file named as: notepad_utf-16le.txt.

5. To see how my text is saved by Notepad, I need to run my HEX dump program on notepad_utf-16le.txt:

```
C:\herong\uni\unicode>java HexWriter notepad_utf-16le.txt
   notepad_utf-16le.hex


Number of input bytes: 170


C:\herong\unicode>type notepad_utf-16le.hex
FFFE480065006C006C006F0020006300
6F006D0070007500740065007200210000
20002D00200045006E0067006C006900
730068000D000A00035751181604F7D59
01FF20002D002000530069006D007000
6C0069006600690065006400020000430
680069006E0065000730065000D000A00
FB966681604F7D5957FE20002D002000
5400720061006400690074006900F00
6E0061006C0020004300680069006E00
6500730065000D000A00
```

Very nice. This is a perfect UTF-16 encoding file using the Little-Endian with BOM format. Those leading 2 bytes represent the BOM flag, which is not part of the text.

Conclusion - The "Unicode" encoding option of Notepad matches the "Little-Endian with BOM" format of Unicode UTF-16 encoding.

Supported Save and Open File Formats

This section provides a quick summary on Notepad saving and opening Unicode files correctly with the BOM character prepended. But Notepad failed to open Unicode big endian files without the BOM character prepended.

Now we learned that Notepad saves Unicode text files in 3 encoding formats:

- UTF-8 format - Text files saved in UTF-8 byte sequences with BOM, 0xEFBBBF, prepended.

- Unicode big endian format - Text files saved in UTF-16 byte sequences in Big-Endian with BOM format.

- Unicode format - Text files saved in UTF-16 byte sequences in Little-Endian with BOM format.

Notepad can open Unicode text files in 5 encoding formats,

- UTF-8 format - Text files opened with encoding format automatically detected.

- UTF-8 with BOM format - Text files opened with encoding format automatically detected.

- UTF-16 (Big-Endian with BOM) - Text files opened with encoding format automatically detected.

- UTF-16 (Little-Endian with BOM) - Text files opened with encoding format automatically detected.

- UTF-16LE format - Text files opened with encoding format automatically detected.

Notepad can not open Unicode text files in UTF-16BE encoding format correctly.

Using Microsoft Word as a Unicode Text Editor

This chapter provides notes and tutorial examples on using Microsoft Word as a Unicode text editor. Topics including opening Unicode text files in 3 encodings: UTF-8, UTF-16BE, and UTF-16LE; saving and opening Unicode text files with the BOM character prepended.

Conclusions:

- Word can be used to edit Unicode text files.

- Word allows you to save Unicode text file in 3 encoding formats, UTF-8, UTF-16 (Big-Endian with BOM), and UTF-16 (Little-Endian with BOM).

- Word can open Unicode text files in 4 encoding formats with encoding automatically detected, UTF-8, UTF-16 (Big-Endian with BOM), UTF-16 (Little-Endian with BOM), and UTF-8 with BOM.

- Word can open Unicode text files in 2 encoding formats with your help to select the encoding manually, UTF-16BE and UTF-16LE.

- The BOM character is the "ZERO WIDTH NO-BREAK SPACE" character, U+FEFF, in the Unicode character set.

What Is Microsoft Word

This section provides a quick introduction of Microsoft Word - a document authoring and publishing tool. Microsoft Word can be used to edit Unicode text files with various encodings.

What Is Microsoft Word? Microsoft Word is a document authoring and publishing tool that is included in the Microsoft Office product suite.

Microsoft Word is mainly used to edit documents formatted for printing. But it also be used to open and save Unicode text files in encoded formats.

Microsoft Word supports at least 4 Unicode encodings: Unicode, Unicode (Big-Endian), Unicode (UTF-7) and Unicode (UTF-8).

Here is a screenshot of Microsoft Word:

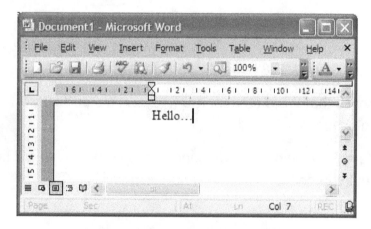

Microsoft Word Screenshot

Opening UTF-8 Text Files

This section provides a tutorial example on how to open a UTF-8 text file with Word correctly by selecting the Unicode (UTF-8) encoding option on the File Conversion dialog box.

Let's try to use Word to open the UTF-8 text file, hello.utf-8, created from the previous chapter first.

1. Run Word and click menu File > Open. The Open file dialog box comes up.

2. Select the hello.utf-8 text file and click the Open button. The File Conversion dialog box comes up automatically. Word detected the encoding to be "Unicode (UTF-8)" and suggests you to use it to read the text file. See the correct text in the preview section in the picture below:

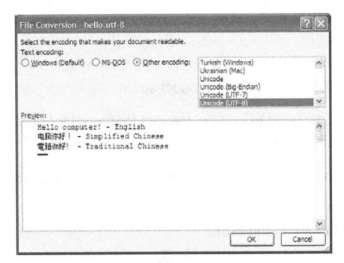

Word Open UTF-8 File

3. Click the OK button. My UTF-8 text file opens in Word correctly.

Very nice. This proves that Word can open UTF-8 text file correctly if the "Unicode (UTF-8)" encoding option is selected.

If you select a different encoding, like Unicode, the UTF-8 text file will be opened incorrectly. Try it out yourself.

Opening UTF-16BE Text Files

This section provides a tutorial example on how to open a UTF-16BE text file with Word correctly by selecting the Unicode (Big-Endian) encoding option on the File Conversion dialog box.

Now let's try to use Word to open the UTF-16BE text file, hello.utf-16be, created from the previous chapter.

1. Run Word and click menu File > Open. The Open file dialog box comes up.

2. Select the hello.utf-16be text file and click the Open button. The File Conversion dialog box comes up automatically. But this time Word failed to detect the correct encoding and suggests you to use the Windows default encoding to read the text file. See the incorrect text in the preview section in the picture below:

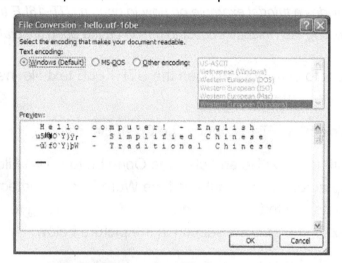

Word Open UTF-16BE File - Bad

3. Click the "Other encoding" radio button and Select the "Unicode (Big-Endian)" encoding from the encoding list. Word now converts the UTF-16BE text correctly. See the correct text in the preview section in the picture below:

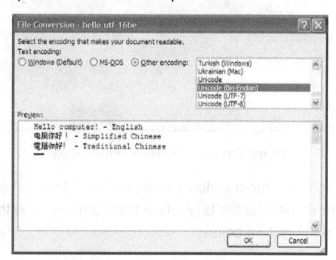

Word Open UTF-16BE File - Good

4. Click the OK button. My UTF-18BE text file opens in Word correctly.

Not too bad. This proves that Word can open UTF-16BE text file correctly if the "Unicode (Big-Endian)" encoding option is selected.

Opening UTF-16LE Text Files

This section provides a tutorial example on how to open a UTF-16LE text file with Word correctly by selecting the Unicode encoding option on the open file dialog box.

In the next test, I want to use Word to open the UTF-16LE text file, hello.utf-16le, created from the previous chapter.

1. Run Word and click menu File > Open. The Open file dialog box comes up.

2. Select the hello.utf-16le text file and click the Open button. The File Conversion dialog box comes up automatically. But this time Word failed to detect the correct encoding and suggests you to use the Windows default encoding to read the text file. See the incorrect text in the preview section in the picture below:

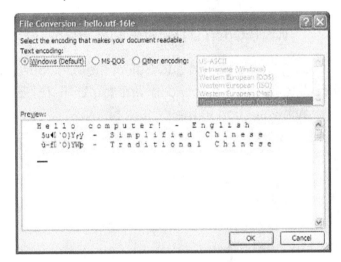

Word Open UTF-16LE File - Bad

3. Click the "Other encoding" radio button and Select the "Unicode" encoding from the encoding list. Word now converts the UTF-16LE text correctly. See the correct text in the preview section in the picture below:

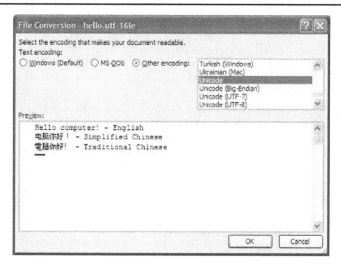

Word Open UTF-16LE File - Good

4. Click the OK button. My UTF-18LE text file opens in Word correctly.

Not too bad. This proves that Word can open UTF-16LE text file correctly if the "Unicode" encoding option is selected.

Saving Files in "Unicode (UTF-8)" Option

This section provides a tutorial example on how to save text files with Nodepad by selecting the 'Unicode (UTF-8)' encoding option on the file conversion dialog box.

After testing the Word open function, now I want to test the save function with the "Unicode (UTF-8)" option.

1. Run Word and open hello.utf-8 correctly with the Unicode (UTF-8) encoding option selected.

2. Click the File > "Save As" menu. The "Save As" dialog box comes up.

3. Enter word_utf-8.txt as the new file name and select the "Plain Text (*.txt)" option in the "Save as Type" field. See the picture below:

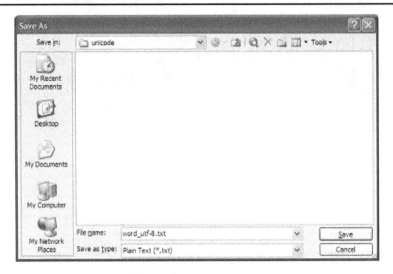

Word Save Text File

4. Click the Save button. The File Conversion dialog box comes up.

5. Click the "Other encoding" radio button and select the "Unicode (UTF-8)" option.

6. Click the OK button. Word saves the text to a new file named as: word_utf-8.txt.

7. To see how my text is saved by Word, I need to run my HEX dump program on word_utf-8.txt:

```
C:\herong\unicode>java HexWriter word_utf-8.txt word_utf-8.hex
Number of input bytes: 107


C:\herong\unicode>type word_utf-8.hex
EFBBBF48656C6C6F20636F6D70757465
7221202D20456E676C6973680D0AE794
B5E88491E4BDA0E5A5BDEFBC81202D20
53696D706C696666656564204368696E65
73650D0AE99BBBE885A6E4BDA0E5A5BD
EFB997202D205472616469746F6F6E61
6C204368696E6573650D0A
```

The UTF-8 text file saved by Word is identical to my original UTF-8 text file except for those 3 bytes in the beginning, "EFBBBF". If we ignore "EFBBBF", we can say that Word saves UTF-8 text file correctly.

Of course, we know why Word prepends "EFBBBF" to the text file. "EFBBBF" is the UTF-8 sequence of the BOM character U+FEFF". See the previous chapter for more information.

Saving Files in "Unicode (Big-Endian)" Option

This section provides a tutorial example on how to save text files with Word by selecting the 'Unicode (Big-Endian)' encoding option on the file conversion dialog box.

In the next test, I want to try the save function with the "Unicode (Big-Endian)" option.

1. Run Word and open hello.utf-8 correctly with the Unicode (UTF-8) encoding option selected.

2. Click the File > "Save As" menu. The "Save As" dialog box comes up.

3. Enter word_utf-16be.txt as the new file name and select the "Plain Text (*.txt)" option in the "Save as Type" field.

4. Click the Save button. The File Conversion dialog box comes up.

5. Click the "Other encoding" radio button and select the "Unicode (Big-Endian)" option.

6. Click the OK button. Word saves the text to a new file named as: word_utf-16be.txt.

7. To see how my text is saved by Word, I need to run my HEX dump program on word_utf-16be.txt:

```
C:\herong\unicode>java HexWriter word_utf-16be.txt word_utf-16be.hex
Number of input bytes: 170

C:\herong\unicode>type word_utf-16be.hex
FEFF00480065006C006C006F00200063
006F006D00700075007400650072002ance1
0020002D00200045006E0067006C0069
00730068000D000A753581114F60597D
FF010020002D00200053006900460070
006C0069006600690065006400200043
00680069006E006500730065000D000A
96FB81664F60597DFE570020002D0020
```

```
00540072006100640069007400690 06F
006E0061006C002000430068006900 6E
006500730065000D000A
```

Very nice. This is a perfect UTF-16 encoding file using the Big-Endian with BOM format. Those leading 2 bytes represent the BOM flag, which is not part of the text.

Conclusion - The "Unicode (Big-Endian)" encoding option of MS Word matches the "Big-Endian with BOM" format of Unicode UTF-16 encoding.

Saving Files in Unicode Option

This section provides a tutorial example on how to save text files with Word by selecting the Unicode encoding option on the file conversion dialog box.

Let's continue to try the save function with the Unicode option.

1. Run Word and open hello.utf-8 correctly with the Unicode (UTF-8) encoding option selected.

2. Click the File > "Save As" menu. The "Save As" dialog box comes up.

3. Enter word_utf-16le.txt as the new file name and select the "Plain Text (*.txt)" option in the "Save as Type" field.

4. Click the Save button. The File Conversion dialog box comes up.

5. Click the "Other encoding" radio button and select the "Unicode" option.

6. Click the OK button. Word saves the text to a new file named as: word_utf-16le.txt.

7. To see how my text is saved by Word, I need to run my HEX dump program on word_utf-16le.txt:

```
C:\herong\unicode>java HexWriter word_utf-16le.txt word_utf-16le.hex
Number of input bytes: 170

C:\herong\unicode>type word_utf-16le.hex
FFFE480065006C006C006F0020006300
6F006D0070007500740065007200210 0
20002D00200045006E0067006C006900
```

```
730068000D000A00035751181604F7D59
01FF20002D002000530069006D007000
6C0069006600069006500640020004300
680069006E006500730065000D000A00
FB966681604F7D5957FE20002D002000
54007200610064006900740069006F00
6E0061006C00200004300680069006E00
6500730065000D000A00
```

Very nice. This is a perfect UTF-16 encoding file using the Little-Endian with BOM format. Those leading 2 bytes represent the BOM flag, which is not part of the text.

Conclusion - The Unicode encoding option of MS Word matches the "Little-Endian with BOM" format of Unicode UTF-16 encoding.

Supported Save and Open File Formats

This section provides a quick summary on Word saving and opening Unicode files correctly with the BOM character prepended. But Word can also open Unicode files without the BOM character prepended with the correct encoding selected manually.

Now we learned that Word can save Unicode text files in 3 encoding formats:

- Unicode (UTF-8) format - Text files saved in UTF-8 byte sequences with BOM, 0xEFBBBF, prepended.

- Unicode (Big-Endian) format - Text files saved in UTF-16 byte sequences in Big-Endian with BOM format.

- Unicode format - Text files saved in UTF-16 byte sequences in Little-Endian with BOM format.

Word can open Unicode text files in 6 encoding formats,

- UTF-8 format - Text files opened with encoding format automatically detected.

- UTF-8 with BOM format - Text files opened with encoding format automatically detected.

- UTF-16 (Big-Endian with BOM) - Text files opened with encoding format automatically detected.

- UTF-16 (Little-Endian with BOM) - Text files opened with encoding format automatically detected.

- UTF-16BE format - Text files can be opened if you select the "Unicode (Big-Endian)" encoding option manually.

- UTF-16LE format - Text files can be opened if you select the Unicode encoding option manually.

Using Microsoft Excel as a Unicode Text Editor

This chapter provides notes and tutorial examples on using Microsoft Excel as a Unicode text editor. Topics including testing to open text files in 3 encodings: UTF-8, UTF-16BE, and UTF-16LE; saving and opening Unicode text files in UTF-16 (Little-Endian with BOM) format.

Conclusions:

- Excel can be used to edit Unicode text files.

- Excel allows you to save Unicode text files in UTF-16 (Little-Endian with BOM) format.

- Excel allows you to open Unicode text files in UTF-8 and UTF-16 (Little-Endian with BOM) formats.

- The BOM character is the "ZERO WIDTH NO-BREAK SPACE" character, U+FEFF, in the Unicode character set.

What Is Microsoft Excel

This section provides a quick introduction of Microsoft Excel - a spreadsheet tool which allows you to enter numerical values or text data into rows and columns. Microsoft Word can be used to edit Unicode text files with various encodings.

What Is Microsoft Excel? Microsoft Excel is a spreadsheet tool which allows you to enter numerical values or text data into rows and columns of a spreadsheet document. Microsoft Excel is included in the Microsoft Office product suite.

Here is a screenshot of Microsoft Excel:

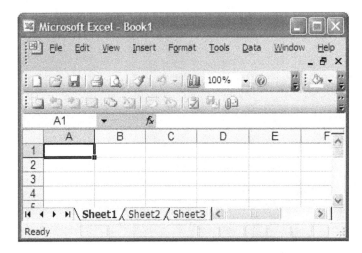

Microsoft Excel Screenshot

Opening UTF-8 Text Files

This section provides a tutorial example on how to open a UTF-8 text file with Excel correctly by selecting the '65001 : Unicode (UTF-8)' encoding option on the Text Import Wizard dialog box.

First, let's try to use Excel to open the UTF-8 text file, hello.utf-8, created from the previous chapter.

1. Run Excel and click menu File > Open. The Open file dialog box comes up.

2. Select the hello.utf-8 text file and click the Open button. The Text Import Wizard dialog box comes up automatically. Excel detected the encoding to be "65001 : Unicode (UTF-8)" and suggests you to use it to read the text file. See the correct text in the preview section in the picture below:

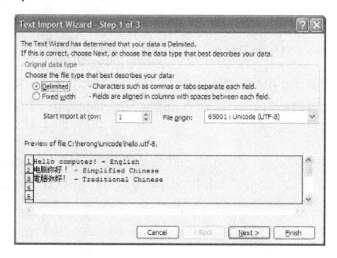

Excel Open UTF-8 File

3. Click the Next button and finish the import process. My UTF-8 text file opens in Excel correctly.

Very nice. This proves that Word can open UTF-8 text file correctly if the "Unicode (UTF-8)" encoding option is selected.

If you select a different encoding, like (65000 : Unicode (UTF-7), the UTF-8 text file will be opened incorrectly. Try it out yourself.

Opening UTF-16BE Text Files

This section provides a tutorial example to prove that Excel can not open a UTF-16BE text file. Its Text Import Wizard only supports UTF-7 and UTF-8 encodings.

Now let's try to use Excel to open the UTF-16BE text file, hello.utf-16be, created from the previous chapter.

1. Run Excel and click menu File > Open. The Open file dialog box comes up.

2. Select the hello.utf-16be text file and click the Open button. A warning message dialog box comes up:

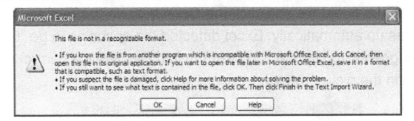

Excel Open File Error

3. Not too bad. The warning message says: "This file is not in a recognized format. ... If you still want to see what text is contained in the file, click OK. Then click Finish in the Text Import Wizard."

4. Ok, let's try to the Text Import Wizard. But Excel does not provide the Unicode Big-Endian encoding in the "File origin" list. It only provides "65000 : Unicode (UTF-7)" and "65001 : (UTF-8)".

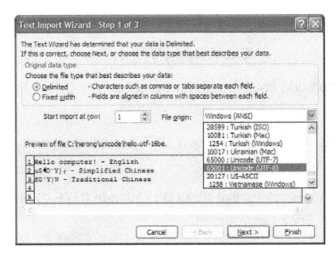

Excel Open File Origin Option

Too bad. This proves that Excel can not open UTF-16BE text files.

Opening UTF-16LE Text Files

This section provides a tutorial example to prove that Excel can not open a UTF-16LE text file. Its Text Import Wizard only supports UTF-7 and UTF-8 encodings.

In the next test, I want to use Excel to open the UTF-16LE text file, hello.utf-16le, created from the previous chapter.

1. Run Excel and click menu File > Open. The Open file dialog box comes up.

2. Select the hello.utf-16le text file and click the Open button. A warning message dialog box comes up.

I tried clicking OK to use the Text Import Wizard. But Excel does not provide the UTF-16LE encoding in the "File origin" list.

Too bad. This proves that Excel can not open UTF-16LE text files.

Saving UTF-8 Text Files

This section provides a tutorial example to prove that Excel can not save a UTF-8 text file. Its Save As Type only supports the Unicode Text (*.txt) encoding.

After testing the Excel open function, now I want to test the save function with the UTF-8 encoding.

1. Run Excel and open hello.utf-8 correctly with the "65001 : Unicode (UTF-8)" encoding option selected.

2. Click the File > "Save As" menu. The "Save As" dialog box comes up.

3. Excel does not provide the UTF-8 encoding in the "Save as type" list. It only provides "Text (Tab delimited) (*.txt)" and "Unicode Text (*.txt)":

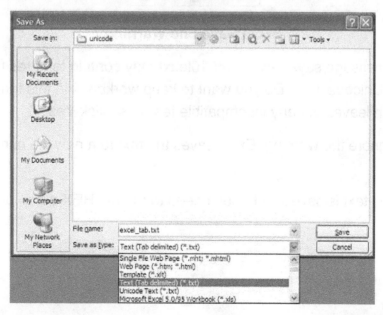

Excel Save File Type Option

Too bad. This proves that Excel can not save UTF-8 text files.

Saving Files in "Unicode Text (*.txt)" Option

This section provides a tutorial example on how to save Unicode text file with Excel using the 'Unicode Text (.txt)' file type option.*

In the next test, I want to try the save function with the "Unicode Text (*.txt)" option.

1. Run Excel and open hello.utf-8 correctly with the Unicode (UTF-8) encoding option selected.

2. Click the File > "Save As" menu. The "Save As" dialog box comes up.

3. Enter excel_utf-16.txt as the new file name and select the "Unicode Text (*.txt)" option in the "Save as Type" field.

4. Click the Save button. A warning dialog box comes up:

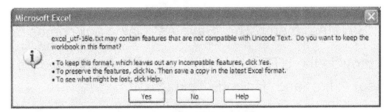

Excel Save File Warning

5. The warning message says: "excel_utf-16le.txt may contain features that are not compatible with Unicode Text. Do you want to keep workbook in this format? To keep this format, which leaves out any incompatible features, click Yes..."

6. Click Yes to ignore the warning. Excel saves the text to a new file named as: excel_utf-16.txt.

7. To see how my text is saved by Excel, I need to run my HEX dump program on excel_utf-16.txt:

```
C:\herong\unicode>java HexWriter excel_utf-16.txt excel_utf-16.hex

Number of input bytes: 170
```

```
C:\herong\unicode>type excel_utf-16le.hex
FFFE480065006C006C006F0020006300
6F006D007000750074006500720021 00
20002D00200045006E0067006C006900
730068000D000A00035751181604F7D59
01FF20002D002000530069006D007000
6C0069006600690065006400200 04300
680069006E006500730065000D000A00
FB966681604F7D5957FE20002D002000
540072006100640069007400690 06F00
6E0061006C0020004300680069006E00
6500730065000D000A00
```

Very nice. This is a perfect UTF-16 encoding file using the Little-Endian with BOM format. Those leading 2 bytes represent the BOM flag, which is not part of the text.

Conclusion - The "Unicode Text (*.txt)" encoding option of Excel matches the "Little-Endian with BOM" format of Unicode UTF-16 encoding.

Opening UTF-16 Text Files

This section provides a tutorial example on how to open a UTF-16 (Little-Endian with BOM) text file with Excel correctly by selecting the 'Windows (ANSI)' encoding option on the Text Import Wizard dialog box.

In the previous section, we saved a Unicode text file in the Little-Endian with BOM format of UTF-16 encoding. Now I want to try to open it back into Excel.

1. Run Excel and click menu File > Open. The Open file dialog box comes up.

2. Select the hello.utf-8 text file and click the Open button. The Text Import Wizard dialog box comes up automatically. Excel detected the encoding to be "Windows (ANSI)" and suggests you to use it to read the text file. See the correct text in the preview section in the picture below:

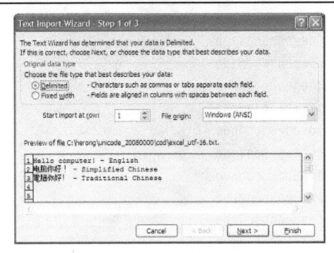

Excel Open UTF-16 File

3. Click the Next button and finish the import process. My UTF-16 text file opens in Excel correctly.

Very nice. This proves that Word can open UTF-16 (Little-Endian with BOM) text file correctly if the "Windows (ANSI)" encoding option is selected.

If you select a different encoding, like (65000 : Unicode (UTF-7), the UTF-8 text file will be opened incorrectly. Try it out yourself.

Supported Save and Open File Formats

This section provides a quick summary on Excel saving and opening Unicode files. UTF-16 (Little-Endian with BOM) is the best format for Excel.

Now we learned that Excel can save Unicode text files 1 encoding format:

- Unicode Text (*.txt) format - Text files saved in UTF-16 byte sequences in Little-Endian with BOM format.

Excel can open Unicode text files in 2 encoding formats:

- UTF-8 format - Text files opened with encoding format automatically detected as "65001 : Unicode (UTF-8)".

- UTF-16 (Little-Endian with BOM) - Text files opened with encoding format automatically detected as "Windows (ANSI)".

Excel can not open Unicode text files in UTF-16BE or UTF-16LE encoding format correctly.

Unicode Fonts

Notes and tutorial examples are provided on Unicode fonts. Topics include characteristics of a font; examples of Unicode fonts; downloading and installing GNU Unifont; running 'Character Map' on Windows.

Conclusions:

* A font is an instance of typeface that defines how glyphs of a character set will be displayed or printed.

* A Unicode font is an instance of typeface that defines how glyphs of the Unicode character set will be displayed or printed.

* "Arial Unicode MS" is a Unicode font that covers 50,377 Unicode glyphs/characters. It is installed as part of the Windows operating system.

* "Character Map" is a nice tool on Windows systems to view and select any glyph from a font family.

What Is a Font

A font can be considered as an instance of typeface that defines how glyphs of a character set will be displayed or printed.

What Is Font? A font is an instance of typeface that defines how glyphs of a character set will be displayed or printed. A font has the following basic properties:

Character Set - Specifies the list of characters that are supported by the font. For example, "Courier" fonts support the ASCII character set for the English language. "FangSong" fonts support the GB2312 character set for the Chinese language.

Size - Specifies the height of glyphs to be displayed or printed. For example, "12pt" fonts display glyphs 12/72, or 1/6, inch high. "32pt" fonts display glyphs half, or 1/2, inch high.

Weight - Specifies the thickness of glyph strokes relative to the font size. For example, glyph strokes in "Bold" weight fonts are thicker than glyph lines in "Normal" weight fonts.

Style - Specifies the slope of glyphs to be displayed or printed. For example, glyphs in "Italic" style fonts are slanted slightly to the right.

Family - Specifies a set of fonts that have same characteristics but different sizes, weights and styles. For example, "Courier" is a font family with fonts like, "Courier 12pt", "Courier 12pt bold", "Courier 12pt bold italic", etc.

The picture below shows some glyphs displayed in 3 fonts of the "Arial" family:

```
┌─────────────────────────────┐
│ Arial 12pt                  │
│                             │
│ Arial 12pt Bold             │
│                             │
│ Arial 12pt Bold Italic      │
└─────────────────────────────┘
```

Sample Glyphs in 3 Fonts of Arial Family

What Is a Unicode Font

A Unicode font is a font that covers a large portion of the Unicode character set to support multiple written languages. For example, Arial Unicode MS and GNU Unifont are considered to be Unicode fonts.

What Is Unicode Font? A Unicode font is an instance of typeface that defines how glyphs of the Unicode character set will be displayed or printed.

Since Unicode character set is so big, 120,737 characters in Unicode 8.0, we do not have any true Unicode font that covers the entire Unicode character set. But we do have some fonts that cover enough Unicode characters to support most commonly used

European, Arabic and Asian languages. Those fonts can be considered Unicode fonts. Below are some examples of Unicode font families:

1. Arial Unicode MS - It covers 50,377 glyphs/characters and produced by Monotype Corporation. The picture below shows some glyphs displayed in "Arial Unicode MS 12pt Bold" font:

Arial Unicode MS 12pt Bold:

ꠍꠍ, ش, 中文, ♚☉

Sample Glyphs in "Arial Unicode MS 12pt Bold" Font

2. GNU Unifont - It covers 63,449 glyphs/characters and produced by Roman Czyborra. The picture below shows some glyphs displayed in "GNU Unifont 12pt Bold" font. They look not as good as the "Arial Unicode MS 12pt Bold" font.

```
GNU Unifont 12pt Bold:
```
ꠌꠍ, ୱ, 中文, ☯

Sample Glyphs in "GNU Unifont 12pt Bold" Font

Downloading and Installing GNU Unifont

A tutorial example is provided on how to download and install GNU Unifont font family on Windows 7 systems.

GNU Unifont is a Unicode font family produced by Roman Czyborra and can be distributed under the GNU General Public License. The latest version of GNU Unifont covers 63,449 glyphs for large number of written languages.

Here is what I did to download and install it on my Windows 7 systems:

1. Go to http://unifoundry.com/unifont.html.

2. Click the link in this statement: "The Standard Unifont TTF Download: unifont-8.0.01.ttf (12 Mbytes)"

3. Save the downloaded file "unifont-8.0.01.ttf" to a local folder like C:\local\font.

4. On Windows Explorer, double-click on "C:\local\font\unifont-8.0.01.ttf". The Windows font installer window will show up.

5. Click the "Install" button. Windows will install the GNU Unifont font family and make it available as "Unifont" to Windows applications like MS Word.

Windows Tool "Character Map"

A tutorial example is provided on how to run 'Character Map' on Windows systems to view glyphs of a Unicode font family.

What Is "Character Map"? "Character Map" is a Windows tool that allows you to view all glyphs/characters that supported by a given font.

Here is what I did to use "Character Map" to locate the glyph of "Georgian Letter Phar" in the "Arial Unicode MS" font family.

1. Go to Windows command search box and enter in "Character Map".

2. Click on "Character Map" in the search result to start it.

3. Select "Arial Unicode MS" from the "Font" dropdown list.

4. Scroll down through the glyph table until you reach "U+10E4: Georgian Letter Phar".

5. Double-click on it to select it, then click the "Copy" button.

Now I can paste it to MS Word, or any application that supports Unicode.

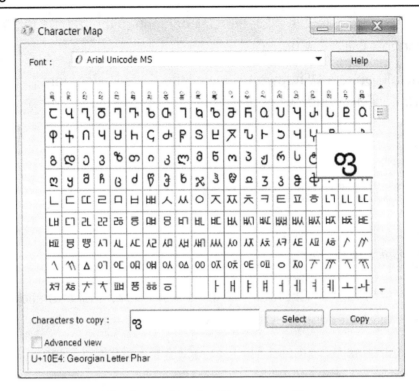

Windows Tool - Character Map

Archived Tutorials

This chapter contains some outdated tutorial notes and example codes from previous versions of this book.

Archived: EncodingSampler.java - BMP Character Encoding

This section provides a tutorial example on how to use 4 different methods provided in Java to encode characters with a given encoding for BMP (Basic Multilingual Plane) characters only.

Java offers 4 methods to encode characters:

- CharsetEncoder.encode()

- Charset.encode()

- String.getBytes()

- OutputStreamWriter.write()

Here is a program that demonstrate how to encode BMP (Basic Multilingual Plane) characters with each of above 4 methods:

```
/**
 * EncodingSampler.java
 - Copyright (c) 2009, HerongYang.com, All Rights Reserved.
 */
import java.io.*;
import java.nio.*;
import java.nio.charset.*;
class EncodingSampler {
```

```
   static String dfltCharset = null;
   static char[] chars={0x0000, 0x003F, 0x0040, 0x007F, 0x0080, 0x00BF,
                   0x00C0, 0x00FF, 0x0100, 0x3FFF, 0x4000, 0x7FFF,
                   0x8000, 0xBFFF, 0xC000, 0xEFFF, 0xF000, 0xFFFF};
   static char hexDigit[] = {'0', '1', '2', '3', '4', '5', '6', '7',
                   '8', '9', 'A', 'B', 'C', 'D', 'E', 'F'};
   public static void main(String[] arg) {
      String charset = null;
      if (arg.length>0) charset = arg[0];
      OutputStreamWriter o = new OutputStreamWriter(
         new ByteArrayOutputStream());
      dfltCharset = o.getEncoding();
      if (charset==null) System.out.println("Default ("+dfltCharset
         +") encoding:");
      else System.out.println(charset+" encoding:");
      System.out.println("Char, String, Writer, Charset, Encoder");
      for (int i=0; i<chars.length; i++) {
         char c = chars[i];
         byte[] b1 = encodeByString(c,charset);
         byte[] b2 = encodeByWriter(c,charset);
         byte[] b3 = encodeByCharset(c,charset);
         byte[] b4 = encodeByEncoder(c,charset);
         System.out.print(charToHex(c)+",");
         printBytes(b1);
         System.out.print(",");
         printBytes(b2);
         System.out.print(",");
         printBytes(b3);
         System.out.print(",");
         printBytes(b4);
         System.out.println("");
      }
   }
   public static byte[] encodeByCharset(char c, String cs) {
      Charset cso = null;
      byte[] b = null;
      try {
```

```
        if (cs==null) cso = Charset.forName(dfltCharset);
        else cso = Charset.forName(cs);
        ByteBuffer bb = cso.encode(String.valueOf(c));
        b = copyBytes(bb.array(),bb.limit());
    } catch (IllegalCharsetNameException e) {
        System.out.println(e.toString());
    }
    return b;
}
public static byte[] encodeByEncoder(char c, String cs) {
    Charset cso = null;
    byte[] b = null;
    try {
        if (cs==null) cso = Charset.forName(dfltCharset);
        else cso = Charset.forName(cs);
        CharsetEncoder e =  cso.newEncoder();
        e.reset();
        ByteBuffer bb = e.encode(CharBuffer.wrap(new char[] {c}));
        b = copyBytes(bb.array(),bb.limit());
    } catch (IllegalCharsetNameException e) {
        System.out.println(e.toString());
    } catch (CharacterCodingException e) {
        //System.out.println(e.toString());
        b = new byte[] {(byte)0x00};
    }
    return b;
}
public static byte[] encodeByString(char c, String cs) {
    String s = String.valueOf(c);
    byte[] b = null;
    if (cs==null) {
        b = s.getBytes();
    } else {
        try {
            b = s.getBytes(cs);
        } catch (UnsupportedEncodingException e) {
            System.out.println(e.toString());
```

```
        }
    }
    return b;
}
public static byte[] encodeByWriter(char c, String cs) {
    byte[] b = null;
    ByteArrayOutputStream bs = new ByteArrayOutputStream();
    OutputStreamWriter o = null;
    if (cs==null) {
        o = new OutputStreamWriter(bs);
    } else {
        try {
            o = new OutputStreamWriter(bs, cs);
        } catch (UnsupportedEncodingException e) {
            System.out.println(e.toString());
        }
    }
    String s = String.valueOf(c);
    try {
        o.write(s);
        o.flush();
        b = bs.toByteArray();
        o.close();
    } catch (IOException e) {
        System.out.println(e.toString());
    }
    return b;
}
public static byte[] copyBytes(byte[] a, int l) {
    byte[] b = new byte[l];
    for (int i=0; i<Math.min(l,a.length); i++) b[i] = a[i];
    return b;
}
public static void printBytes(byte[] b) {
    for (int j=0; j<b.length; j++)
        System.out.print(" "+byteToHex(b[j]));
}
```

```
    public static String byteToHex(byte b) {
        char[] a = { hexDigit[(b >> 4) & 0x0f], hexDigit[b & 0x0f] };
        return new String(a);
    }
    public static String charToHex(char c) {
        byte hi = (byte) (c >>> 8);
        byte lo = (byte) (c & 0xff);
        return byteToHex(hi) + byteToHex(lo);
    }
}
```

Note that:

- If the same encoding is used, all 4 methods: encodeByString(), encodeByWriter(), encodeByCharset() and encodeByEncoder(), should return the exactly the same byte sequence.

- getEncoding() is used on OutputStreamWriter class to get the name of the default encoding.

- There is no way to know the name of the default encoding on String class.

- There is no default instance of Charset and Encoder.

This tutorial example program only works for BMP characters. The newer version of this program presented earlier in this book can support both BMP and supplementary characters in range of 0x0000 - 0x10FFFF.

References

List of reference materials used in this book.

- *Unicode Code Blocks - Herong's Notes*, Herong Yang, herongyang.com/Unicode-Code-Blocks

- *GB2312 Tutorials - Herong's Tutorial Examples*, Herong Yang, herongyang.com/GB2312

- *The Unicode Standard Version 13.0 Core Specification*, The Unicode Consortium, unicode.org/versions/Unicode13.0.0/UnicodeStandard-13.0.pdf

- *The Unicode Standard Version 11.0 Core Specification*, The Unicode Consortium, unicode.org/versions/Unicode11.0.0/UnicodeStandard-11.0.pdf

- *What is Unicode?*, Unicode, Inc, unicode.org/unicode/standard/WhatIsUnicode.html

- *The Unicode Standard: A Technical Introduction*, Unicode, Inc, unicode.org/unicode/standard/principles.html

- *Unicode Code Point Charts*, Unicode, Inc, unicode.org/charts

- *Unicode Public FTP Site*, Unicode, Inc, ftp://ftp.unicode.org/Public/

- *Universal Character Set*, en.wikipedia.org/wiki/Universal_Character_Set

- *UTF-8, a transformation format of ISO 10646*, 1998, tools.ietf.org/html/rfc2279

- *UTF-16, an encoding of ISO 10646*, 2000, tools.ietf.org/html/rfc2781

- *Unicode Standard Annex #19 - UTF-32*, 2002, unicode.org/reports/tr19/tr19-9.html

- *Comparison of Unicode encodings*, en.wikipedia.org/wiki/Comparison_of_Unicode_encodings

- *GB18030-2000 - The new Chinese National Standard*, Sun Microsystems, 2002, http://www.sun.com/developers/gadc/technicalpublications/articles/gb18030.html

- *HZ-GB-2312 - ASCII Printable Characters-Based Chinese Character Encoding for Internet Messages*, Wei, et al, 1995 faqs.org/ftp/rfc/rfc1842.txt

- *CJK Character Sets and Encoding Forms*, Gyula Zsigri, 2002, zsigri.tripod.com/ fontboard/cjk/charsets.html

- *A Brief History of Character Codes*, Steven J. Searle, 2002, tronweb.super-nova.co.jp/characcodehist.html

- *Japanese text encoding*, Ping, 1996, lfw.org/text/jp.html

- *Notes on CJK Character Codes and Encodings*, Ross Paterson, 1995, ftp:// ftp.cuhk.edu.hk/pub/chinese/ifcss/software/info/cjk-codes/index.html

- *Unicode 11.0.0*, The Online Edition, 2018, unicode.org/versions/Unicode11.0.0/

- *Unicode 10.0.0*, The Online Edition, 2017, unicode.org/versions/Unicode10.0.0/

- *Unicode 9.0.0*, The Online Edition, 2016, unicode.org/versions/Unicode9.0.0/

- *Unicode 6.0.0*, The Online Edition, 2010, unicode.org/versions/Unicode6.0.0/

- *The Unicode Standard, Version 5.0*, The Online Edition, 2006, unicode.org/ versions/Unicode5.0.0/

- *The Unicode Standard, Version 4.0*, The Online Edition, 2003, unicode.org/ versions/Unicode4.0.0/

- *The Unicode Standard, Version 3.0*, The Online Edition, 1999, unicode.org/book/ u2.html

- *Unicode Character Ranges*, JRX, jrgraphix.net/r/Unicode/

- *Unicode HOWTO*, python.org, docs.python.org/3/howto/unicode.html

- *Supplementary Characters in the Java Platform*, Oracle, oracle.com/us/ technologies/java/supplementary-142654.html

- *Java® Platform, Standard Edition & Java Development Kit Version 11 API Specification*, Oracle, docs.oracle.com/en/java/javase/11/docs/api/

- *Java Platform, Standard Edition 7 API Specification*, Oracle, docs.oracle.com/ javase/7/docs/api/

Unicode Tutorials
Herong's Tutorial Examples

v5.32, 2024

Herong Yang
HerongYang.com/Unicode

This Unicode tutorial book is a collection of notes and sample codes written by the author while he was learning Unicode himself. Topics include Character Sets and Encodings; GB2312/GB18030 Character Set and Encodings; JIS X0208 Character Set and Encodings; Unicode Character Set; Basic Multilingual Plane (BMP); Unicode Transformation Formats (UTF); Surrogates and Supplementary Characters; Unicode Character Blocks; Python Support of Unicode Characters; Java Character Set and Encoding; Java Encoding Maps, Counts and Conversion. Updated in 2024 (Version v5.32) with minor changes.

HerongYang.com
30+ Tutorial Books
Computers / Programming